AMAZING
GRACE

AMAZING GRACE

The Life of John Newton and the
Surprising Story Behind His Song

BRUCE HINDMARSH

CRAIG BORLASE

W PUBLISHING GROUP

AN IMPRINT OF THOMAS NELSON

Amazing Grace

© 2023 Bruce Hindmarsh and Craig Borlase

Published in Nashville, Tennessee, by W Publishing, an imprint of Thomas Nelson.

Published in association with the literary agency of WTA Media, LLC, Franklin, Tennessee.

Thomas Nelson titles may be purchased in bulk for educational, business, fundraising, or sales promotional use. For information, please email SpecialMarkets@ThomasNelson.com.

Unless otherwise noted, Scripture quotations are taken from the King James Version. Public domain.

Scripture quotations marked ESV are taken from the ESV® Bible (The Holy Bible, English Standard Version®). Copyright © 2001 by Crossway, a publishing ministry of Good News Publishers. Used by permission. All rights reserved.

ISBN 978-4003-3404-9 (audiobook)
ISBN 978-1-4003-3403-2 (eBook)
ISBN 978-1-4003-3401-8 (HC)
ISBN 978-1-4003-3402-5 (TP)

Library of Congress Control Number: 2022947112

Printed in the United States of America
23 24 25 26 27 LBC 5 4 3 2 1

To Charles Morris

Contents

Swissair flight 111 was en route from New York to Geneva on the evening of September 2, 1998, when it suddenly plummeted 2,400 meters into the Atlantic Ocean off the coast of Nova Scotia, killing all 229 people on board. The tiny tourist village of Peggy's Cove was immediately transformed into a command center for the police, Coast Guard, and other emergency officials. Shocked family members arrived to look out over the waves that held their loved ones. An army chaplain went to the water's edge and offered to pray with the grieving family of a nineteen-year-old California student. He led them in prayer, and then the family started to sing a hymn in four-part harmony, and then followed this with "Amazing Grace." The chaplain noticed that all the rescue workers and onlookers were transfixed by the scene. Everyone stopped until they were done. He added, "Things like that were going on all day—amazing grace in the middle of incredible sorrow."

It was on those same North Atlantic seas 250 years earlier that John Newton, the author of "Amazing Grace," first cried out to God for mercy in the midst of a storm that threatened to kill all on board a foundering ship bound for England. Newton wrote "Amazing Grace" some years afterward, when he was settled at a parish church in the English Midlands as an Anglican minister, but the hymn has endured through two and a half centuries and has become today a powerful symbol for many people of hope in the midst of tragedy.

The hymn has figured prominently at moments of intense national grieving in America. After the space shuttle *Challenger* burst into flames on television in 1986, the American people heard "Amazing Grace" played at the memorial service for the astronauts. After a domestic terrorist exploded a bomb at an Oklahoma City federal building in 1995, killing 168 people, "Amazing Grace" was again carried from church services by television news programs. The memorial Mass for John F. Kennedy Jr. in July 1999 concluded with the singing of "Amazing Grace" as well.

In 2001, immediately after the terrorist attacks on September 11, a spontaneous candlelight vigil began in Union Square, and people started again to sing "Amazing Grace." This did not just happen in New York. "Amazing Grace" was sung at both formal and ad hoc memorials across the United States. This song continues to be sung at commemorations of the event and in other times of public tragedy and private grief. Examples abound. "Amazing Grace" is, as one critic observed, the "spiritual national anthem" of America.

In Canada, on November 20, 1998, at the memorial service for Michel Trudeau, the son of former prime minister of Canada Pierre Trudeau, who was killed in a skiing accident, "Amazing Grace" was played on bagpipes. Two years later, on the anniversary of the Columbine High School shootings in America, a student at a high school in Orléans, near Ottawa, stabbed four fellow students and a school instructor before giving himself up to the authorities. In the pandemonium and shock afterward, a number of Pentecostal students gathered at the front of the school, held hands, and began to pray. They were soon joined by other students, Christian and non-Christian alike. Spontaneously, they began to sing "Amazing Grace." That was when the media noticed the prayer circle and the cameras focused on the forty to forty-five students. It was on the national news that evening.

Perhaps even more remarkably, this song that was written by a former slave trader has been taken up by African American congregations and made their own. This was true before and after emancipation in America. "Amazing Grace" became a song of personal testimony. It was gospel music greats like Mahalia Jackson, who offered the song to a wider audience yet. She recorded "Amazing Grace" for Apollo Records on December 10, 1947. Her soulful version of the hymn was played on the radio in the immediate postwar years and helped to move "Amazing Grace" into the popular consciousness once and for all. It was there to be sung during the civil rights movement. It was there to be sung during the Vietnam years. It was there for everyone who needed a prayer for grace in times of pain and unrelenting wretchedness.

After a white supremacist shot and killed nine African Americans in Charleston, South Carolina, at an evening Bible study on June 17, 2015, including the politician and senior pastor of the Mother Emanuel AME Church, Rev. Clementa Pinckney, President Barack Obama gave the eulogy for the slain pastor. In the middle of the president's remarks, he paused. He wasn't sure whether he would do this, but when the moment came, it seemed right to him. President Obama began singing "Amazing Grace." He knew the congregation would join in with him right away, and they did. It was a powerful moment.

Where do we find hope today in the midst of deep divisions in society and violent disagreements? Where do we find hope for the human condition? Where do we find hope for all the griefs and sorrows that threaten to undo our lives? Perhaps we need to look again at the perennial message of "Amazing Grace." Perhaps here we might find a renewed hope that however difficult the troubles in our lives, however deep our personal shame and regret, however dark the evil that stalks the earth, there is a mercy that is deeper yet, a forgiveness that makes all the difference, and a power for reconciliation greater than ourselves.

The 250th anniversary of the writing of the hymn by John Newton is a fitting occasion to discover the remarkable story behind the song and to learn something of the dramatic life of its author. In this story is a message of grace for us all today—one we need to hear, now more than ever.

When John Newton wrote his autobiography in 1764 at nearly forty years of age, he published it anonymously with an almost tabloid-style title: *An Authentic Narrative of Some Remarkable and Interesting Particulars in the Life of* *********. The cover promised a faithful retelling of what would be some extraordinary experiences. It did not disappoint.

The book you hold presents Newton's story retold for another generation. Like his autobiography, it also seeks to be an "authentic narrative," taking the real drama of his life and filling out the scenes based on the hints he gave us and from what we can reconstruct from other historical sources. For example, in the first chapter we combine the facts of eighteenth-century Wapping, where Newton grew up, with his own recollections to recreate his early boyhood as vividly as it would have been for him (including a dead body). We want you to have a front-row seat to his biography as it unfolds in real time.

Importantly, though, we have used our imagination not only to add color or to embellish an old story, but also to enter as fully as possible *into* John Newton's mind and his world at every stage. We have based these imagined scenes on the many sources he left us, including his autobiography, diaries, logbooks, letters, and extensive published writings. To this has been added research into other contemporary sources and the considerable scholarship available on Newton and his times. His world was as real as ours—just as tactile, visual, and audible—and we want you to feel this.

This has meant creating fictional but plausible dialogue and conceivable episodes to fill in the biographical facts and framework as realistically as possible and represent the inner life of Newton and his contemporaries. Sometimes the dialogue is verbatim, drawn from Newton's letters and other writings, and at other times it is imagined. But this is not a novel. It is a dramatized biography with the feel of a film or live play. It is important for readers to know that the principal narrative, the chronology, and all the proper names (people, places, ships) and documents (hymns, letters, books, minutes of meetings, etc.) follow the sources exactly. In fact, in several places we have quietly corrected details that were mistaken in earlier biographies. We have included some notes on sources for each chapter at the end of the book and a short bibliography for those who would like to dig deeper into the historical record. In drawing upon original sources and manuscripts, we have modernized spelling, punctuation, and capitalization, where this would otherwise be a distraction for the reader.

In the end, we hope the result for you as a reader will be a lively story that captures the deep truth of John Newton's life, one that places you right in the midst of the drama. If you feel what he felt—see him striding proudly along the River Thames in his sea coat, feel the slap of the salty sea spray on his cheeks in the North Atlantic, and hear the clop of horse hooves on the cobbles of the eighteenth-century city streets he walked—then you have actually gotten a little closer to Newton. Our hope is that this will be another "authentic narrative" of some still very "remarkable and interesting particulars" in the life of John Newton.

When you read about Newton's dramatic life, immersing yourself in it like this, you will inevitably pause now and again to compare his experience to yours. He made some very foolish decisions. Well, so have we. He did things that were shameful. We hate to admit it, but so have we. He fell punch-drunk in love as a young man and often acted stupidly, and, oh, we can remember those moments in our own lives. And so on.

And then as Newton descends into deeper darkness, ready even to kill himself and capable of murder, we are left to ponder the times we, too, have been desperate and felt that all hope was lost. Even harder, when he sinks so low as to enter into the slave trade, unaware at the time of how evil this was, we may have to pause and ask ourselves whether we could be capable of something like that.

Most of all, though, as Newton finds mercy and forgiveness, and when he shows remorse and grows in wisdom and love, we may be inspired to think, *If there was grace for him, maybe there can be grace for me too.* A story like Newton's invites us to be honest about failure, about wretchedness, about the things to which we once were blind. If "Amazing Grace" means anything, it means this.

In Newton's story we see a clear illustration of the fact that nobody comes to Christ painlessly or all at once—that though the gift of grace is freely given, none of us receive the gospel without having to go deeper, well beyond the moment of initial conversion. The more we become aware of how deep is our need for grace, the more we understand how precious a gift it is.

And so Newton's story is a journey of discovery—a journey we must all travel ourselves. In Newton's life we see a parable of how we need grace far more than we initially thought. We see that we have been complicit in things that have been deeply hurtful to others. We see that the older we get, the more we need grace, for the closer we get to the light, the more impurities show up. Maturity means knowing more and more how much we stand in need of God's grace, and walking therefore with humility and gentleness, just as Newton did. But at every step, God is at work, calling us home to himself. There is room enough yet in this story for us all.

Part 1

'Tis grace has brought me safe thus far

John Newton woke up blind in the darkness, and lay there, perfectly still. His eyes were half welded shut, crusted tight by sleep. The house was locked up in silence too. Nobody was stirring. Not the old couple who slept in the room next door. Not the maid in the scullery below. Yet there was something calling to him, something propelling him out from under the stiff cotton blanket that his father had brought back from one of his many voyages. Alexandria? Venice? John could never remember. Not that it mattered. He kicked the blanket off and crept out into the darkness. After all, it wasn't every day a boy got to see a dead body.

The room was unfamiliar to him, but he did not light a candle. His exit had been well planned, and he had laid all his clothes out in order the night before. His yellow woolen stockings, his dark velvet breeches with buckles at the knees, the long coat that people said made him look like a miniature version of his father. He dressed in careful silence so as not to wake anyone else in the house. He had no idea what they would do if they found him up so early. They were kind folk, good people who were friends of his mother. There was a chance they would have no issue with a six-year-old boy going out onto the streets of London on his own like this, but it was better not to find out. The adventure was worth the risk. After all, they said the dead body swinging from the gallows was one of the most notorious pirates of his day.

By the time he felt his way downstairs and stepped out into the street, the sky was just beginning to shift from inky black to bruised gray. John knew the streets of Wapping far better than the house that had been his home ever since his mother's health deteriorated, and he moved swiftly along the narrow lanes and alleyways. He passed silent, lifeless houses that he knew were home to joiners and shipwrights, to coopers and caulkers and boat makers—men with whom his father had business, whenever he was home. John was careful to keep away from the sewage that flowed in streets toward the Thames and knew well enough how foul the stench would become as the summer's day progressed. People called it the *evil odor*, and it was one of the reasons he had chosen to make his trip at first light, when the air was still cool. There were other reasons, too, like the fact that at such an early hour the crowds would not have formed. He could get close to the body, close enough to see it in all its tortured glory. And if he needed to, he could run away without any trouble.

Within minutes he rounded a corner and came face-to-face with the Thames. He stopped. The river was full, just like it always was, but no matter how many times he had seen the same view, it was impossible not to pause and stare at the floating empire laid out before him. There were hundreds of ships of all sizes and styles on the river. Brigs and snows, one-mast sloops and two-masted schooners, all designed and modified for their particular purpose. For every one of these merchant vessels, there were four or five barges nearby. Some would be ferrying customs officials on board to ensure the correct taxes were paid, some ferrying supplies to those waiting to leave. There was no limit to the power of British maritime trade.

John ran his eyes over the scene, taking in every change since the day before. He knew some of the ships by name, and those he did not he could read like words in a hymnbook. Having grown up with a captain for a father, it was easy to tell apart the ones trading around the North Sea or the Mediterranean from those that went as far as the East Indies, bringing back silk and spices. The simplest to spot were the ships that headed south to the Guinea coast of Africa before taking their human cargo across the Atlantic and following the trade winds home, loaded with sugar, rum, and tobacco. With their fenced-in quarters on deck and nets to prevent people jumping overboard, the slave ships were the only ones that looked like floating prisons.

John stood and stared long enough for the sun to rise clear in the sky. When he felt light on his face, he turned away. Upstream was the rest of London, but he had no interest in Parliament or palaces. Downstream was where he wanted to go. Eventually he'd join his father and make it out to the ocean and then on to the rest of the world. But first it would take him to the place he had spent the last day thinking about: Execution Dock.

John walked as far as he could along the Thames before the road led him away, passing shops and yards that were as familiar to him as the warmth of his mother's embrace. The moment the air turned stale with the smell of sweat and tobacco, rum and sugar, John's pace quickened. Even though his father was far away on a run to the Mediterranean and wouldn't return for months, John had no desire to linger near Captain Newton's favorite coffee shop. Instinct had taught him that the loud-mouthed, fierce-eyed men who frequented it were best avoided whenever possible.

The sea trade was full of big men with loud voices and foul tongues who ruled by fear. John had been surrounded by them from the day he was born. He had learned how a man who had power out there on the sea, who commanded crews of mutinous sailors and navigated the dangers of pirates and privateers, demanded to be treated with deference and respect. Even in his own home. Especially by his only son. So John had grown up knowing only ever to call his father "sir," to always walk ten paces behind him when in public, and to quickly drop his eyes to the ground the moment his anger flared. Fear was the one gift his father had given John. That and the stiff cotton blanket that was about as comfortable as sleeping beneath a canvas sail.

John approached Execution Dock for the second time in as many days. Yet now, early on Sunday morning, the place could not have looked more different from the way it had the previous afternoon. On Saturday there had been thousands of people gathered, a giant press of cheering, happy onlookers. The crowd surged the length of the dock, overflowing onto the stairs that led to it and onto the nearby riverbanks for a better view. John had tried to cleave his way through them, but it was no use. He had soon found himself crushed on all sides like a ship trapped in the ice in the frozen north. He had been forced to retreat farther downriver and follow events as best he could from a distance.

The procession had sounded more like a carnival than a death march, with people cheering and laughing all around as it made its way from the Tower of London down past London Bridge. John had only caught a glimpse of the high court marshal walking at the front, carrying a silver oar as a sign of his authority. Behind him, John guessed, was the cart with the doomed man and the chaplain should the condemned wish to confess his sins.

He hadn't been able to see the man approach the gallows. Hadn't been able to hear whether he addressed the crowd or not. But he had heard the shouts and cries of delight throughout the crowd as soon as the rope snapped tight, and the noose did its work.

Now, with the entertainment of the previous day over, John was almost alone as he approached the dock. The tide was out, revealing a wide track of dark mud, rock, and human waste that led down to the water's edge. Up by the shore, yet close enough to be almost completely covered by the river at high tide, were the gallows. John had passed them almost daily when there was no body and had often stared at the greasy algae that clung to the timbers, making them look like they belonged to a long-abandoned shipwreck. He'd asked his mother plenty of questions, like why the gallows were built down so close to the water or what kind of crimes the men committed who were punished there. Her answers were always brief as she hurried him along.

There was no mother to stop him now. There were no crowds for him to fight through, either. No press of bodies that threatened to throw him from the stairs that led from the street down to the waterside. There were only the gallows, a handful of people milling around on the steps nearby, and a body turning slowly at the end of the rope—where it would remain until three tides had washed over it.

John inched closer. Only one tide would have risen and fallen since the man was hanged the previous afternoon, but the body already was marked by the hours it had spent underwater. His hair spread in worm-like tendrils over his pale, bloated face. His eyes were locked open, staring out at the sky. There was a growing stench of seawater, sewage, and decay around him, and the man's filthy, wet clothes were steaming in the morning sun. For a moment it looked as if he was being slowly burned to death.

"Lord, have mercy on the poor sinner," said a soft voice at John's side. He turned to see a man staring up at the rope, his head slowly shaking from side to side. Beyond him was a woman, her eyes narrowed and sour.

"There be no mercy for the likes of him," she spat. "Nor should there be. Sinners get what they deserve."

The man opened his mouth as if to speak, but the sound of nearby church bells left him silent.

It was John's cue to leave, but he took one last look up at the body before turning to the man beside him, and he asked the question that had been with him all morning. "Was he really a pirate?"

"No," the man frowned. "He was no pirate. He was a captain."

"A captain what became a thief," added the woman. "Don't matter who you are, your sins will find you out. Thems that deserve it always end up swinging from the rope."

John took the back route over the road, passing by the timber yard and out onto Gravel Lane. The streets were no longer empty, especially outside the churches where knots of well-dressed people gathered and greeted one another politely. He sped up and danced around those waiting outside the parish church that his father attended whenever he was home. John never much liked it there. It was almost impossible for him to sit still for so long while the congregation chanted one long, slow psalm after another. When his attention wandered—which it always did—his eyes would wander. He'd take in the statues carved from marble and paintings in their gilded frames. They made him want to get out of the heavy pew and run, even more than the singing.

His mother's church was a different story altogether. The building itself looked different, with no paintings and no statues, just plain walls and a simple pulpit at the front. His mother had tried to explain why there was such a contrast between his father's church and hers—something about Jesus forgiving people who truly repented of their sins—but to John it only ever came down to the songs. Instead of droning through metrical psalms that left him trying to suppress his desire to yawn, in his mother's church—the Dissenting Chapel as she called it—the songs made him feel alive. People sang with real feeling, like the words meant something. And the music! He heard one of the old men in the congregation say that when these tunes were first introduced, Queen Elizabeth herself had called them "Genevan jigs." These were the sort of tunes that made him want to stand up and smile, to throw his head back and bellow the words as loudly as if he was standing on deck, calling to shore.

The chapel service was just about to start as John nodded good morning to the old couple in whose house he had been staying for the past weeks. He slipped into the pew that he usually shared with his mother. Five Sundays had passed since she last sat next to him. Five weeks in which he spent Monday to Saturday trying not to think about the way she looked before she left the city to stay with friends in the country, where the air would be better for her. But here, on Sunday in the chapel, with nothing but empty space beside him, he was powerless to hold the thoughts back. It was bittersweet.

As the room stood to sing the first hymn, he smiled. It was one of his mother's favorites, and his too. He sang,

O God, our help in ages past.

The words rose strong and warm within him. It wasn't hard to imagine his mother standing right beside him. Her thick skirts that swayed as she sang. Her eyes smiling as her high, clear voice guided him along the melody.

Our hope for years to come.

The way she would place her hand on his shoulder and draw him closer to her. The way she would squeeze tighter whenever they reached the words she liked best of all.

Our shelter from the stormy blast,
And our eternal home.

The song over, the congregation returned to their pews, ready for the sermon. The minister's opening words were not what John expected.

"There is a body swinging down by the river today," he said, his slow Scottish baritone rolling through the chapel. "Many saw him die. Many even cheered when he did. But I tell you this: we are none of us so very different from that sinner hanging at the dock. We are all fallen from God. We have all broken his covenant and transgressed his laws. None of us have a rag to cover our nakedness, so wretched are we."

The minister paused and the room froze in the silence. Head bowed, John felt as if the dead man's eyes were staring right at him.

"And yet, all of us have the hope of the gospel. All of us can be redeemed. The meanest and vilest of sinners may fly to Christ for mercy."

The minister carried on for some time, talking about how the law was a schoolmaster to bring people to Christ. John understood little, but he felt much. A twist in his stomach, a catch of breath in his throat as if the air was suddenly weaker. Or maybe it was stronger; he couldn't tell. But he knew without a doubt that he was relieved when the sermon was finally over and the singing resumed. And when he stood again to open his mouth and let his voice flow out, it was as if his mother was right there beside him.

A week later John woke up later than usual. It was already light outside and there were voices downstairs. He recognized the old couple, but there was another voice speaking that was unfamiliar to him. He tried to make out what they were saying, but the voices were quiet and muffled. With the parlor occupied, he would struggle to slip out of the house unnoticed, not that it mattered. He was feeling excited. His seventh birthday was fourteen days away, and he had it on good assurance that his mother would be well enough to receive him. He lay in bed imagining what it would be like to board the coach and ride east to the fields of Kent. How he would polish the buckles on his breeches and shoes beforehand and be sure to shake every last mote of dust from his coat. He would tell her all the news from London, recount what he could of the sermons that she had missed on Sundays. He might even tell her about the great crowds that had gathered for the man who had been hanged, though he would report it all as rumor instead of firsthand experience.

As soon as he was dressed, John skipped downstairs and into the parlor, still a little lost in his thoughts. The old couple were sitting down, but it was the presence of a stranger standing by the fireplace that brought him back to himself. He was younger than John's father but looked just as somber.

"Master John," said the old lady, not looking at anyone in particular. "This is Mr. Catlett. It is with his family in Kent that your mother has been staying these past few weeks . . ."

Her voice trailed off. Nobody spoke.

John decided to hide his confusion and offer a small bow, the kind he had seen his father give whenever he saw a wealthy merchant down by the docks. "I am pleased to meet you, Mr. Catlett. Am I to travel with you to see my mother today? Is she recovered early?"

There was no reply. He searched for an answer in the faces of the only people he knew, but they offered none. All eyes were on the man by the fireplace. His were fixed on the floor.

"Your mother," said Mr. Catlett, his voice barely making it out from his throat. "She passed."

John Newton—now a strong-shouldered fifteen-year-old with four sea voyages to his credit, freshly returned from eight months spent working in the office of one of the most esteemed merchants in the whole of Alicante, Spain—stepped down from the carriage that had paused at the entrance to the farmhouse. He hauled his heavy wooden sea chest that contained almost all his worldly possessions onto the grass and felt the dread rise within him like bile. He was back home, returning once again to stay with his family. Never before had he felt so much like an unwelcome stranger.

The farm at the village of Aveley in Essex belonged to his stepmother's family. So, too, did his father. They had married within two years of his mother's death, not long after his father had returned home from his Mediterranean run to be told that his wife had died from consumption. Almost as soon as Captain Newton sold up, married, and moved out of London, John had been sent away to boarding school. After two years of beatings at the hands of harsh schoolmasters, he had returned to the farmhouse to find that his stepmother had given his father another son, with one more child on the way. It was as though he had been replaced. The farm at Aveley had never been John's home, and the people living within its walls had never really been his family.

John left the sea chest on the grass, briefly considered whether he should knock on the door, then walked inside. There was nobody around. It was only when he opened the door to the parlor that he found someone, a young servant girl he did not recognize—and who clearly did not recognize him. She glanced up from the fireplace that she was clearing out, shot him a mildly terrified look, and fled out the door. He was alone in a house where he had always felt alone.

It was late afternoon in high summer and all the windows were closed tight, turning the air stale and lifeless. John stood in the silence and instantly remembered how much he disliked the farm at Aveley. The room was full of furniture and paintings that served only to remind him how little he belonged. Half of the furniture was his stepmother's—the plain writing table, the clock, the painting of a hunting scene in the rolling countryside. These things all looked as if they had never belonged anywhere else, as if the house had been built around them. But they clashed mightily with the rest of the room, which was full of ornately upholstered chairs, an oversized gilded mirror, and various wall hangings and oddments that could have been purchased only in some dusty, distant port. These were furnishings John could easily recall from his childhood home in London. There were other items, not present, that he remembered too—a painting of his mother's father, a delicately made wooden box in which she kept her most treasured letters, and her Bible with its dark leather cover wrinkled from use. None of these were in the parlor now. Nothing about the room gave any hint that his mother had ever existed. John's pulse quickened and he resolved to ask his father about these missing mementos as soon as he saw him.

The floor outside creaked just as the door opened and his father entered.

Captain Newton had always been an imposing figure. His chest was as broad as a forty-gallon barrel of rum, his stare as fierce and fixed as the noonday sun. He never merely walked into a room; he would often pause at the threshold, as if it was his first time on the deck of a ship of which he had just taken command. Even when he had secured every last scrap of attention from those present, he would wait. He would hold the silence. Even the stillness of the air was his own, along with the room and the people and anything else that he desired. Only when the room submitted, when the conquest was over, would he speak.

"You look tired, John."

John's mouth opened but no words came out.

"What? Are you not well?"

"No," he said, though it sounded more like a cough than a real word. "Quite well, Father. Thank you."

Captain Newton broke off his gaze and swept across the room. "Sit with me," he said, carefully rearranging his long coattails as he settled himself in the ornate chair. "The letter. From the Spaniard. I trust you have it?"

John reached into his pocket and handed it over, the taste of bile in his mouth even stronger now.

The letter was addressed to Captain Newton, written by his friend, the merchant to whom John had been apprenticed for much of the last year. It was an account of John's time in Alicante, a report of his work as a junior clerk in his warehouse, and—John assumed—an explanation of why the twelve-month posting was terminated at eight.

Captain Newton's face was locked rigid as a death mask. For over a minute his eyes slid across the page, betraying nothing of the letter's contents or his reaction to them. As his father neared the end, John wondered whether the verdict might not be so bad after all. Until something on the page snagged the old captain's eyes. John saw them hover, narrow, then lift slowly and lock upon his own.

"Well," said Captain Newton, exhaling slowly. It was neither a question nor an invitation, and the word died in the air.

John knew better than to speak to his father without being addressed directly, so he stood in silence, eyes on the intricately woven rug at his feet. The room felt even more crowded and stuffy.

"The Spaniard is a wise man," said Captain Newton. "He is a good man too. And, I should like to add, the Spaniard is also a partner of mine in trade. We have conducted business together over many years. He is not a man who makes mistakes."

Captain Newton held the letter almost at arm's length, staring at it as if the ink was still wet and he was worried about it staining his clothes or the furniture.

"The Spaniard writes that you lack restraint. He describes your behavior as unsettled. He even suggests that you have developed a foul mouth capable of profanity, which actually concerns me less. It was always your mother who cared about profanity, not I. My cares have always been that you are too easily lost in your own thoughts. Too easily swayed by childish passions."

Captain Newton's stare shifted from the letter to his son.

"Nothing he writes surprises me. Nothing, that is, apart from his closing statement. He writes that, as a man of business and trade, you are sorely lacking. He judges that you are not worthy of the Newton name."

There was a tremor in his voice, and though John knew he should not look up, he could not resist. His father's face was flushing red, the vein in his temple visible now. The mask was finally breaking.

"I bred you to the sea," spat Captain Newton, abandoning any attempt to hold his anger in check. "I took you with me, shared my cabin and my food with you. I taught you how to live aboard, how to survive. I even dared hope that one day you might become a captain yourself. And yet you return from Spain in disgrace, sent home because of your failings. Have *I* failed in some way? Is the error *mine*?"

John's head was heavy and his mouth was dry. He stared at the fireplace. He felt suffocated, like all the air had left the room. How good would it feel to pick up the heavy iron poker and use it to smash all the windows, one by one? He could almost taste the clean, fresh air flowing in.

He looked back toward his father, who was still presenting the letter like a lawyer at court. Still staring hard at him. Still burning red.

"No, sir."

In the season that followed John's return to Aveley, little happened. His father spent several months away on a run across the North Sea, and John tried his absolute best to avoid interaction with anyone else in the house. He soon mastered the art of living as a ghost. He found that days could pass without him seeing either his stepmother, her parents, or either of his two half-siblings. All he had to do while he was in the house was stay quietly in his room reading, only leaving when he was sure that there was nobody around. On the one occasion each week when he was forced to be in their presence—the Sunday morning visit to the parish church—they did not trouble him with conversation.

Outside the house, however, John was anything but silent. He knew several of the boys in the village and would happily spend hours in their company when they had time to spare. They were a tough bunch, the wild sons of cowmen, dockhands, and drovers, and most of them were apprenticed to their fathers' trades. John knew they saw him as something different, even exotic, and he played his role with flair. They would listen in silence as John shared stories from his most perilous voyages with his father, and they'd snigger like little boys at the description of the whores who lived near the merchant offices in Alicante.

Best of all they liked it when John would bring a pair of hunting horses from the farm's stable block and lead them on frantic gallops over fields and down narrow lanes until the horses' eyes rolled white and the boys felt sick from fear.

When winter was just beginning to ease, there emerged some news that was even more interesting than stories of Spanish whores or Turkish pirates. The British Admiralty was preparing for war with Spain, and a naval frigate, ready for battle, had been spotted at anchor in the Thames just a mile and a half south of the village. Being the nautical expert of the group, John led an expedition one Sunday afternoon so that the boys could see it for themselves.

When they reached the bank, John saw that she was even more impressive than he had imagined. With two decks, seventy cannon, and three fully rigged masts as tall as any he had ever seen, she dwarfed every other vessel on the river. All five boys watched in silence as the crew busied themselves rowing boats and ferrying supplies from the dock on the far side of the river.

After an hour or two, as they were preparing to leave, one of the sailors rowed toward them, fighting against the strong currents that were well-known in this reach of the river. He shouted for their attention and asked whether they would like to go on board. They all agreed heartily, and he told them to return the following Sunday at noon. He would row them over for a tour.

All week long John thought about the frigate. He considered making up an excuse to miss church on Sunday morning but did not like the idea of having to talk with the family any more than was strictly necessary. No, he could attend church and still make it to the frigate in time.

Church, for once, ran long. When it was finally over, John fled the church-yard as quickly as he could and ran the mile to the river at full speed. He arrived on the bank in time to see the sailor pulling on the oars with all four of his friends already aboard, laughing and cheering him on. He was too late.

John's anger and frustration mounted as he looked after them but froze the moment he heard a shout from the boys and saw the longboat pitch violently over. He had no idea what caused it, but he watched in horror as all of his friends and the sailor himself were thrown powerfully from the boat. The boys were floundering in the water. Like John himself, none of them could swim, and even if they could, the currents would have been too powerful. Within less than a minute, his best friend was gone and most of the others.

The death of his companions had a powerful effect on John. For weeks he was overwhelmed by the realization that his life had been spared by his simple decision to go to church that morning. His near escape occupied his every waking thought, and a good deal of his dreams too. He had been spared by doing his religious duty, saved by his obedience. There was only one possible response—to be the most saintly Christian possible from now on. He must redouble his religious seriousness. For several years he had oscillated between sin and conscience, but no more. He was fifteen, but he would live, for all intents and purposes, like a monk.

To anyone looking on from a distance there was little difference in his outward behavior. He did stop stealing horses from the stable, but mostly he spent his time avoiding people. To those living at the farm, the changes were more obvious. He stopped eating meat. He could often be heard sobbing in his room, bemoaning his sins, and when he wasn't weeping, he could be observed praying or reading Scripture endlessly, day and night. He hid away like a hermit for almost two years, hoping that if he could only avoid all distraction, perhaps then he would become holy.

"Enough!" Captain Newton started shouting the moment he threw open John's door and swept back the curtains. There was no pausing on the threshold to take command of the room, no attempt to coerce attention by a prolonged silence. This was an all-out attack, a broadside from twenty cannon at close range, designed to overwhelm and achieve immediate surrender. "You shall cease this nonsense immediately!"

John said nothing. He hadn't, in fact, been praying much and it had been days since he last opened his Bible. His religious resolves had given way to a more general moroseness. He had been sitting alone, shivering in the cold and staring at the dwindling fire in the grate, counting down the hours until the short winter's day was over and he could go back to bed.

"Please," said Captain Newton, waving a letter. His voice was quieter, almost gentle now. "I have news for you. I inquired of a friend of mine whether he might have a position for you. And I have now heard back."

John kept his head low, not bothering to make eye contact. The captain did not seem to notice and carried on.

"His name is Joseph Manesty and he is a merchant in Liverpool. I have never sailed for him, but I have it on good authority that his business is sound. He writes that he will take you on. He is offering you a position in Jamaica."

John looked up.

"Yes, I thought that might be of interest to you. A few years in the West Indies and you'll forget all about these wretched winters."

"What is his trade? I know nothing of the land."

Captain Newton smiled. "Sugar."

The word instantly made the room ten degrees warmer. There wasn't a person in England who had not heard of the wealth of the sugar planters. Theirs was a world of gilded carriages and lavish estates, and there were rumors that some planters had become wealthier than the king himself.

"Yes," said Captain Newton, clearly pleased with the prospect for his son and speaking more quickly now. "That is the beauty of what Manesty proposes. You need know nothing of the sugar trade at first, for he is offering you a job as an overseer of slaves. But he writes that if you prove yourself shrewd and hardworking, he will make you a full planter within five years. If you make a success of that, then you can return to England, buy a fine estate, and perhaps even enter Parliament. It is a path to success and the chance of a lifetime. What do you make of it?"

The idea of becoming a wealthy man grew on John and grew quickly. Sugar was the gateway to everything that was good in the world, and only a fool would turn his back on so great an opportunity. There was another aspect to Manesty's offer that appealed almost as much as joining the ranks of the sugar rich, though John barely admitted as much to himself, let alone his father. The stirrings were there, all the same. Ever since he had seen his friends die on the Thames, he had tried so hard to suppress his wild and reckless appetites, but those willful passions had refused to die. If he was in Jamaica for five years or more, away from all the restraints of home, he could indulge whatever pleasures he wanted. He would be free to live as he pleased. True, it did not fit with the idea of being a pious, respected churchman, but after so many months of trying to live free from sin and to avoid all temptation, he was exhausted. Sin was everywhere, wasn't it?

Within days the plans were in motion. Letters were sent to and from Manesty, confirming John's acceptance of the post and arranging the dates for his arrival at the offices in Liverpool and his subsequent departure for Jamaica at the start of the new year. It gave John just one more month of life in Aveley. He was seventeen years old, and he counted down the days like a prisoner awaiting freedom.

With less than a week to wait before his departure for Liverpool, John was preparing to run an errand for his father the next morning. It was a half day's ride toward and across the river to pass through the town of Chatham in Kent and deal with some business matter or other in Maidstone, and the distraction was welcome. Captain Newton had just given him the papers to take on his journey when a letter addressed to John arrived at the farm door.

He did not recognize the handwriting, but the name of the sender brought him back to a world that was long forgotten. It was from Mrs. Elizabeth Catlett, the woman who had nursed his mother in her final weeks and whose husband had delivered the news of her death. She was inquiring after his health and news of his life in general and made it clear that, if ever he should desire, he would be more than welcome to visit them at their home in Chatham.

The coincidence struck John immediately. What were the odds of the invitation arriving the very day before he was due to pass directly by the Catletts' house? Surely it was too implausible a coincidence to ignore. Yet John's first instinct was to do precisely that. More than a decade had passed since his mother's death. The thought of returning to the house where she died and dredging up old feelings troubled him.

Still, there was something about the letter. The way she talked so lovingly about his mother. There was a warmth in her turn of phrase, a kindness and gentleness that flowed from her pen to the page. It called to a part of him that had been buried for years.

Though the morning was fresh and the sky clear when he left the farm, by the time John arrived at his destination at noon the weather had turned sour. When he finished his father's business and mounted the horse to begin his journey home, the rain stung at his cheeks. He was tempted to forget all about his plan to visit the Catletts. It would be better just to stay in his saddle and battle through the wind and the rain until he was home again.

In the end, he decided to stop, if only briefly. The closer he got, however, the more the feelings of loss over his mother's death returned to trouble him. He could hear the blood rushing loud in his ears as he stood at the door and knocked. He was nervous. His throat became dry and shut tight as he heard the sound of people moving within. But the moment the door opened, he forgot all about the cold and the long journey home and the rain that was dripping down his back. The anxious feelings evaporated like summer morning mist as Elizabeth Catlett gasped, reached out for both his hands, and let the tears flow down her face.

"Oh my!" she cried, her eyes dancing with joy. "Oh, my dear boy! I would know you anywhere, John Newton!"

She stepped out and embraced him there in the doorway, with the rain falling on them both. She held him for the longest time before sweeping him inside to meet the family who had already gathered in the hallway, eager to welcome him in. First he met John, the eldest son who was eleven, and Mary, who was two years older and balancing baby George expertly on her hip. She said hello and explained that everyone in the family called her Polly before retreating from view. Sarah—aged four—demonstrated her very best attempts at a pirouette, while two-year-old Susanna looked on from behind her mother's skirts. Even though the sight of Mr. Catlett briefly transported John back to the day he discovered that his mother had died, his broad smile, firm handshake, and warm words of welcome quickly erased any trace of sorrow from John's heart. The effect was so instant and so powerful that it almost seemed like magic.

From the very moment that the front door closed beside him, John felt like he had slipped into another world. How could this be? Chatham was only half a day's ride from the farm, but here in the home of the Catlett family, everything had been renewed. Silence had been replaced by laughter, closed doors and windows thrown wide-open. They were elegant, polite, and well-mannered to be sure, but it was a home of living, breathing, shouting, dancing people, not a house of statues. John could feel himself coming alive.

For an hour or more the conversation tumbled and rolled around him like music. Mrs. Catlett—who insisted that he call her Aunt and Mr. Catlett Uncle—peppered him with questions about his life one minute, then told him stories the next, stories that he had never heard before of her childhood friendship with his mother. John Catlett was fascinated by John's tales of life at sea, and Sarah finally executed her pirouette without stumbling.

Soon John was invited through to the dining room and sat among the family around a large table bathed in candlelight. The stories came faster now, the laughter louder and longer. He had no memory of what food he ate that evening, but he knew it to be better than any meal he had ever enjoyed before in his life.

They returned to the parlor after they had eaten and played cards for an hour or more. John was given baby George to hold when Sarah knocked her father's glass of port over. No one seemed to mind, and it surprised him how much he enjoyed holding the baby as he slept in his arms.

"Well, John," said Uncle George (as Mr. Catlett insisted John called him) once the children were sent up to bed, "it is far too late for you to be riding home tonight. You will stay with us, of course."

"And not just tonight either," said his wife. "Stay a week, stay two if you can. We have plans for a visit to the market at Maidstone next Saturday. Is there any reason you are needed back in Aveley before then?"

John did not hesitate, did not even pause to consider mentioning Liverpool or Joseph Manesty or five years in Jamaica that would transform him into a wealthy man. "None at all," he said. "None at all."

That night he lay awake and listened to young John Catlett snore gently on the other side of the room. The last time he had slept in the company of another person he had been sailing back from Spain. He had lain awake then most nights as well, his mind fearful of what his father would say to the letter he carried with him from the merchant who had just dismissed him as an unruly apprentice.

Now, two years on and in the home of the Catletts, John could not have felt more different. There was no fear, only wonder. How could two families be so different? How could the air in one house be so stale and old, while in the other it was sweeter than any he had ever tasted? How could his father have kept him away from this family for so many years?

He suspected that he knew the answer to that question. At one point in the evening Elizabeth had hinted that she and George had disapproved of the speed with which Captain Newton had remarried. John had no idea if they had expressed any such misgivings to his father, but he knew that if they had, Captain Newton would not have taken it kindly.

Yet instead of brooding over these thoughts and nurturing resentment, John lay awake feeling happier than he had felt at any other point in his life. About the source of this there was no doubt or confusion whatsoever.

It was Mary—or, Polly, as her family called her.

She had captivated him from the very first moment he saw her in the doorway. The way she had greeted him with such a natural smile, radiating something that came from deep within, only then to look away bashfully. Her kindness to her siblings, the way she praised young Sarah for every ballet attempt. Her capacity for laughter and singing and joy of all kinds. She was more alive than any person he had ever met. Yet she carried herself with all the poise of one who moved easily in social circles well beyond his own.

He lay there with his heart beating, bone-tired but soul happy. Sleep was impossible, but it did not matter a bit. He wondered whether she would let him call her Polly in the morning, and how he might go about asking. It was a delicious conundrum to contemplate, the kind that left him smiling in the darkness until he closed his eyes and slipped into the imagined world of a life together with the girl who was even now sleeping just a few feet away in the next room.

Even before he could bring the subject up himself the next day, Polly insisted that John address her like everyone else in the family. His blushes matched hers and he happily agreed, just as he agreed to Aunt Elizabeth's invitation that he stay a while longer.

John was still with the Catletts when they visited the market at Maidstone the following Saturday. He was with them when they attended church the day after that as well. All through the following week he stayed on at their house, taking walks in the afternoon and playing cards in the evening. He learned to laugh as they laughed, to tease and be teased in return, and to remember what it felt like to be treated with genuine, unabashed affection. The great gloom that surrounded his father was nowhere to be seen in the Catlett home. There was only ever warmth and light and love.

In time, however, John accepted that he had to leave. After three weeks in their company, he saddled his horse—who had grown fat from the lack of exercise—and then he moved from one family member to the other, saying his goodbyes, until he became mortally tongue-tied as Polly was left, standing before him.

Hours later he was just as silent, though with a whole different range of emotions, as he stood before his father and the captain roared and raged like the fiercest of typhoons ever known. This time it was not love that choked back John's words. It was fear, the only emotion that his father ever seemed to evoke in him.

John stood and listened as his father ranted about how he had thrown away the best opportunity a young man could ever hope to receive. His father shouted about the embarrassment of having had to inform Joseph Manesty that John had gone missing. "There is no chance of a passage to Jamaica now, I tell you. And even if there was, do you really think Manesty would trust you after what you have done?"

John said nothing. No matter, his father's anger. He was busy thinking of Polly, secretly congratulating himself for having executed his plan so well. He had stayed long enough for the plan of spending five years in Jamaica to be well and truly destroyed. Whatever came next, he would surely be able to see his beloved again soon.

Captain Newton was still shouting. "And your stepmother," he hissed. "Think of what you have done to her. She has been sick with worry all this time, afraid that you were murdered or press-ganged by the navy to fight another of this nation's infernal enemies."

John risked looking at him, but he dared not say what was in his head—that he was surprised that Captain Newton's wife had even noticed his absence, let alone feared for his safety.

There was yet more shouting, but his father was slowly winding down. John dropped his eyes and felt himself slip back down into the gloom that permeated every inch of the house. He waited for his father to end, knowing that he would have no choice other than to accept his punishment, come what may.

"You need discipline," Captain Newton said, his mouth flecked with spittle. "And there is one place that you can be sure to receive it."

John looked hard at his father, wondering whether he was about to tie him to the door and give him forty lashes with the cat-o'-nine-tails as if he was some errant sailor.

Captain Newton paused, breathed deep and exhaled slowly. "It is time you served as a common sailor. There will be no more sailing with me. No more enjoying the privileges of the captain's cabin. No more of the quarterdeck for you. You need to be below deck, with the ordinary seamen. There, among the unruly wretches, you will learn to behave. For if you do not, the suffering you will endure will scar you forever."

In less than a week John was precisely where his father wanted him—on a merchant ship preparing to head out into the English Channel, bound for the Mediterranean and the distant ports of Antioch, Tyre, and Alexandria. He would be away for months, perhaps even as long as a year. But if Captain Newton hoped that fear of harsh life aboard would shock his son into a change of attitude, he was mistaken. The way John saw it, no matter how long the run lasted he would still be reunited with Polly far sooner than if he had taken up a position in Jamaica for Manesty.

The hope of being reunited with Polly shone bright within him, bright enough to see John through his first days on board. As the ship was readied for sea—with repairs being carried out, supplies taken in and stowed, and sails, yards, and topmasts raised—twelve-hour days stretched to thirteen, fourteen, and longer still. Each night he returned to the forecastle—the low, damp space in front of the mast where the crew slept—and collapsed into his hammock that swung inches away from his fellow common sailors. He was exhausted, and the voyage had yet to begin.

Despite the fact that John had only a handful of voyages to his name, he soon discovered that sailing with his father had given him his sea legs and taught him the basics of sailing, though shielding him from the realities of life among the lowest on the ship whose place was before the mast. When the ship finally weighed anchor and land slipped from view, it became clear that blisters, exhaustion, and claustrophobia were only part of the challenge ahead of him. The crew became restless and unruly, and at times the forecastle felt more like a tavern on the verge of a drunken brawl than a place for weary men to rest and recuperate.

More than once a crew member crossed a line and encountered the wrath of the captain. When it became clear that his preferred punishment was woolding—where the first mate wrapped a rope around the guilty sailor's head and tightened it until his eyes popped out—the crew's behavior improved instantly.

For much of the voyage south along the coast of France and then Spain, John kept his head down and his mouth shut, something that his father had given him ample opportunity to practice. By the time they passed through the Strait of Gibraltar and into the Mediterranean itself, he started to thaw. He became a little less shy, joining in with the sea shanties that they sang while they worked. He stopped trying to suppress his laughter when the songs got a little bawdy. He turned his back on whatever faint traces of religion remained within him, and once more gave himself over to pursuing a life without much thought of God. In Rotterdam on his last voyage with his father, he had picked up a book entitled *Characteristicks* by a "freethinking" philosopher. It became his new Bible. It worked like a poison, emboldening him to live his own life on his own terms, like being captain of his own ship. In time he took up swearing again, returning to one of the vices that had landed him in so much trouble during his months as an apprentice back in Spain. Soon John was cursing and blaspheming and sounding more and more like a regular sailor. By the time they arrived at the island of Zakynthos off the coast of Greece, and the sailors made plans for their night in port, he was considered to be part of the crew enough to be invited to go whoring with them.

John declined. He said that he was happier taking a watch and staying on board. He didn't try to explain about his feelings for Polly or talk about his determination to remain chaste for her. He just left the men to go and walked the deck as night fell, listening to the distant sounds of a harbor town coming to life.

When his four-hour watch was over, John retreated to his hammock. The others wouldn't return to the ship for hours, and he appreciated the fact that for once, the smell and heat of the forecastle were almost bearable. He was tired, and not just because of staying awake for the watch or all the hard work of loading and unloading that was involved whenever a merchant ship arrived in port. His fatigue went deeper, right down to his core, to his very soul.

The dream started immediately.

At first, it was unremarkable. He was alone, on deck, midway through a watch while the ship was docked outside Venice. It was as if his mind was every bit as tired as his body, and instead of creating a whole new dreamworld it could only summon the energy to rewind John's life a few weeks, to the scene of the ship's last anchorage.

When a stranger appeared on the far side of the deck, John knew he was dreaming. When the stranger invited John to approach and see something precious, John knew that he had to obey.

"Here," said the stranger, extending his hand. "See what I mean?"

John could feel his sleeping pulse quicken. It was the most beautiful ring he had ever seen, a thick band of gold with a bright ruby glowing in the center. When he was finally able to peel his eyes from it, he noticed that the man was staring at him, smiling.

"Take it," he said, grabbing John's hand and placing the ring in his palm. It was heavier than John imagined it would be, and so much warmer. "Preserve it carefully, mind. While you do so, you will be happy and successful. If you lose it or part with it, you must expect nothing but misery."

John looked up but the man was gone. The deck was empty again and he returned his gaze to the ring. It was like holding a whole world in the palm of his hand, an entire star compressed into one simple, beautiful ring—a ring that had power beyond any he had ever heard of.

"That," said a voice he did not recognize, "is a fine jewel." John looked up to see a different stranger standing before him. He was staring at the ring, his eyes wide in appreciation.

"Yes," said John. "And as long as I have it, this ring will make me happy and successful."

The man's eyes snapped up to John's. He frowned momentarily before his face broke out in a wide smile. "A magic ring?" He was laughing now. "Are you sure? That sounds like a fantasy to me."

John was instantly humbled and closed his hand. "Well, I am not sure. There was a man and he said that it had power and then he gave it to me. But . . . I . . . I do not know where he is now. If we find him, I can have him explain to you what he meant."

The second man smiled and waved his hand in front of him as though he was clearing smoke.

"No. You do not need to find that man to know the truth about that ring. You should throw it away."

The idea made John recoil. "I shall not. This ring is . . ."

The words wouldn't come.

He looked in his hand again. It was a fine ring, but he suddenly felt foolish for believing it was anything else.

"Very well," he said, hurling the ring far away from the ship into the pitch black of the ocean night.

The sound of the ring hitting the water was loud and low. The rumble grew quickly until it was as loud as any storm John had ever sailed through. He looked up to see distant mountains engulfed by flame.

"You fool," sneered the second man. "That ring held God's mercy. Now that you have thrown it away there is nothing for you in life but the fires of judgment."

For a moment John was alone on deck. His hand empty, his eyes locked on the flames in the distance. Then he heard someone approach. It was the first man. John's chest gripped tight with fear. Bitter acid rose in his throat.

"Peace," he said, his eyes kind as he looked at John. "Peace. Tell me, if you have the ring in your possession again, do you think you will be wiser? Will you hold on to it and not be swayed by those who would lead you astray?"

John nodded. It was all he could do. He watched as the man smiled, climbed onto the deck rail that ran around the ship, and dived into the water.

As soon as he returned, the distant flames died out. Apart from the sound of water dripping from the man's clothes, the deck was silent and perfectly still. The man stood, eyes fixed on John, and opened his hand to reveal the ring again.

John grabbed for it, but the man was too quick. He pulled it back out of reach and shook his head. "No. If you took it now, you would only throw it away again. I will hold it for you instead. Whenever you need it, I will produce it on your behalf. But you must choose how you are to live. Will you pursue virtue, or will you turn your back on it?"

"Yes," said John, his voice as loud and as clear as the flames that had lit up the night sky. "I choose virtue. All my days I shall choose it."

Chapter 3 ———— Consequences (1743-1745)

In the weeks following his appointment to the Royal African Company, Captain Newton often found himself in a reflective mood. Most evenings he would sit alone in the parlor, inhaling the sweet aroma orbiting the glass of Madeira wine, and let his eyes grow heavy with pleasure. The wine reminded him of so many places, so many people. Crowded ports where strange tongues filled the air. Stone-faced merchants who would thrust a dagger in your side if they could profit enough from your death. A lifetime of maritime adventure held in his hand. His new position was an enviable one, and a significant promotion for which there had been much competition. After all, for almost a century the Royal African Company had been one of the key tools in the expansion of English trading interests on the West African coast. But taking the job largely put an end to his days at sea. There would be no more breathless runs down past Gibraltar. No more outwitting the scurrilous Turks that patrolled the eastern waters. For any man with salt water in his veins, choosing when to end his career was the greatest challenge of all. Not everyone succeeded. But with war at hand Captain Newton was sure that his timing had been perfect.

One evening early in December, Captain Newton was sitting before the fire, glass in hand, eyes closed. There were no warm memories, however. There was only frustration.

Yet again John had visited the Catletts—just as he had for the first time exactly one year previously. Yet again John had failed to return when he said he would. Yet again Captain Newton had arranged a job for his son, which John had completely ignored.

It troubled him that John had chosen to visit the Catletts as soon as he had returned. A more loyal son would have spent more time with his real family first, paid his respects to his father and stepmother and inquired about the health of his sister and brother. But John had been infatuated with the Catletts ever since he met them. Perhaps it was little wonder he disappeared as soon as he hauled his sea chest through the door.

Yet Captain Newton knew the Catletts well enough. Even when his first wife was alive, he had never much cared for them. Of course, he was gracious enough to acknowledge their kindness in taking her in and nursing her in her final weeks. But it seemed all too clear that they never approved of his new marriage.

And now any visit of his son to their house seemed to spell trouble. He wondered what they were saying about him in his absence. Were they undermining his attempts to direct his son's course in life?

At the sound of the front door closing, Captain Newton opened his eyes. He listened carefully to the feet crossing the hallway, easily recognizing them as John's. He heard the lad pause outside the parlor door and felt the boy's hesitation as he approached.

Captain Newton could put up with only a few seconds of silence.

"Hurry up and get in here!"

He watched John slide in through the door. The boy's eyes were locked on the floor, his body backed up tight against the wall.

He studied his son. Spending the best part of a year at sea had left its mark on John. His hands were slightly calloused and his shoulders—scrawny little stumps inherited from his mother—were finally starting to fill out. But that same wistful, childish air still clung to him.

"You are late," Captain Newton said, holding his anger in check. "Several days late."

The boy said nothing but kept his gaze on the floor.

"You are aware that you missed an appointment that I arranged for you?"

Captain Newton waited for his son to answer. With every second that passed in silence, he felt the anger rise within him. He closed his eyes and tried to force it down, but the rage was too strong.

"I ought to disown you," he spat. "Cut you out like a rotten timber from an otherwise sound hull."

The moment he had said the words, he regretted them. He opened his eyes again, saw his son standing sheepishly in front of him, and felt the anger subside. He emptied the glass with one swallow and held it out for his son.

"Oh," said the boy, scrambling to action and fumbling with the bottle. "Yes, sir."

Captain Newton was on the verge of telling the boy to leave when something gave him pause. The lad looked nervous. He was fiddling unnecessarily with his shirt sleeve—the ridiculous red-checked shirt of a common sailor that he insisted on wearing still. Perhaps another voyage would be required.

"I have been thinking, sir," John said as he handed his father a second glass.

Captain Newton tensed. He studied his son, ready to repel any heresy that the Catletts had fed him.

"Sir, I should like to command my own ship one day."

Captain Newton was momentarily lost for words. It was an unfamiliar sensation, and not one that he particularly enjoyed. Then he remembered the Spaniard's letter. What was the phrase? *Not worthy of the Newton name.* That still tasted like venom.

Another sip of wine and he searched the boy again, this time with even more care. There was something else about him that had changed, something more than flesh and muscle and the putting away of childish behavior. After a lifetime spent at sea, Captain Newton knew better than any man how to spot the strong from the weak. Did he detect now in his son a certain posture, a way of holding himself with more confidence? It was only vague, and he had certainly never seen it before. But it was there, and no mistake.

"So your time in the Mediterranean was not a total failure."

John's feet shifted, but his jaw was up. A little pride looked good on the boy.

"No, sir. It was . . . I believe it was of benefit to me."

"Good. Well. You should know that the challenge is great for any man, let alone one who has squandered the good lessons that his father has tried to teach him these last few years."

John flinched, but only briefly. He took in a deep breath and looked directly at his father. "Yes, sir. I have not been a good pupil. But I should like to rectify that. The Newton name is much respected at sea, and I believe that I could become a good captain one day. Perhaps even a great one."

Captain Newton smiled. It wasn't confidence that he had spotted. It was arrogance. "Good," he said, draining his glass and relishing every warm tendril as it traveled down his throat. "Good."

Though he had been unable to see it at the time, John had now finally accepted that his father's decision to send him on his Mediterranean run was a shrewd one. He had departed with his heart full of hope that he might one day marry Polly but no real plan for how to become a worthy suitor. Those months at sea had been exhausting, and it had been humiliating to have to serve at the lowest possible rank. But the experience had opened his eyes to a world of opportunities.

It had also changed how he saw his father. To take charge of a ship was a great honor. To do so with the level of authority and discipline that Captain Newton commanded was truly remarkable. For the first time in his life, John began to see him not as someone to be feared but respected. Perhaps even as someone to be emulated.

John's resolve to follow in his father's footsteps was strong. In the days and weeks that followed, he talked with his father frequently, always listening carefully as Captain Newton outlined the many pitfalls to avoid and the rare opportunities to take hold of. These conversations were long and slow, and Captain Newton seemed intent on always reminding John of the dangers at sea. He spent hours listening to old stories of Barbary pirates who would enslave and sell any man they captured. There were long lectures about the dangers of being press-ganged into His Majesty's navy as well, especially with Spain and France stirring for war and the navy in need of thousands of extra men. But John did not mind. The more they talked, the more assured John felt in his father's company. The fear that had always been present whenever John stood before him ebbed away. The more they talked, the more he believed that he was not just capable of captaincy but destined for it.

He needed it. His last visit to the Catletts had been a success, but not a wholehearted one. The family had welcomed him back warmly, with the younger children swarming over him and wrestling him to the ground. He told them about his travels, weaving epic tales of adventure and drama on the high seas. His account of surviving a treacherous storm was so vivid—and his accompanying actions as he held the young boy on his lap were so vigorous—that at several points young Master George turned a distinct shade of green. But his tongue was still heavy as an old iron anchor whenever he was in Polly's presence, and there was something about the way Uncle George inquired of John's career intentions—a coldness in his eyes as he asked, "And shall you continue to sail as a common sailor?"—that had left John experiencing an unfamiliar yet distinct flush of irritation. Though there was much left unsaid, it was clear that if John were truly to make a success of himself at sea, Uncle George would most certainly approve.

With the winter storms keeping the Mediterranean ships away, opportunities for finding a voyage on which he could serve were slim. Yet John was keen, and when he wasn't visiting the Catletts or talking with his father, he spent as much time as possible by the Thames, carefully studying every ship that he saw. Most belonged to the navy. At the quayside all the talk was of the mortifying defeat of the British when they engaged the combined fleet of the Spanish and French off the south coast of France. And there were rumors that France was making plans for an invasion. In John's lifetime, war had never felt closer.

While John listened dutifully to his father, and even grew so bold as to ask him questions about how he had achieved such success, he did not heed every piece of instruction given. Especially when it came to what he wore. His father had long warned him against wearing his sailor's shirt and heavy sea coat, questioning why on earth he would want to look like a common sailor.

"You should be humiliated to dress so humbly," Captain Newton had said, time and time again. "Why would you advertise your status as a merchant seaman? Besides, these days only a fool would make himself such an easy target. You know there are gangs of navy thugs rumored to be wandering the towns in search of men they can press into service?"

"Yes, sir." John had heard the rumors, too, but he also knew precisely where the press-gangs were operating. They were far away in Rochester and Gravesend, where the merchant sailors lived. Aveley was farming country. They would never venture as far west as this. But he did not dare contradict his father. "I shall dress more wisely," he'd added.

Heedless of his father's advice, John was walking near the Thames one late February morning, enjoying the view of the ships and looking every inch the sailor that he was, head held high, feeling very much like a captain in training, when he heard the sound of metal chains rattling behind him and realized all of a sudden that he had made a terrible mistake.

"You. Turn around." He didn't recognize the voice that issued the command, but there was no mistaking its authority. It was full of confidence, daring him to disobey.

John turned and saw three men. The one in the middle had a face as weathered as the Atlantic coast. On one side was another who had a neck like a bull and was holding a crude cudgel in his hand. The third was smaller and holding the chain. It had thick iron manacles on either end. As soon as they saw his shirt, all three smiled.

"What ship do you serve?" asked the one with the empty hands.

John froze, momentarily dumb.

"You're obviously a sailor. What ship do you serve? Show us your papers."

"I . . . my father . . . he is Captain Newton . . . I . . ."

John's voice burned away like early morning mist. The man turned and shared a smile with his two colleagues. "Your father could be the Duke of Gloucester for all I care. If you're not already serving, then you're fair game."

Within seconds John's wrists had been seized, twisted, and thrust into the manacles. The iron bit right onto the bones of his wrists. John felt the anger rise within him and tried to wrestle away.

"None of that," said the bull-necked man as he grabbed the chain and twisted it in a way that sent even more pain through John's arms. It forced him to bend forward, like an old and lame beast beaten by some mighty weight.

It was no use. From then on John accepted that he was beaten. He did not resist as they marched him through the streets and did not look up as he sensed onlookers staring at him. They took him inside a local inn and waited while the innkeeper's wife unlocked the heavy wooden door to the empty storeroom in the back. John stood silent and meek, walking into the room when they told him to, and then sitting on the cold stone floor as directed while they removed his chains.

John shivered and closed his eyes. He listened carefully as the three men stood outside, discussing where they should go in pursuit of their next victim. When he was sure they had gone, he called out, hoping that someone would hear.

"Quiet," came the immediate reply. The voice was muffled by the thick wooden door, but John was sure it belonged to the innkeeper's wife.

"Please. I have been pressed. I need to get out."

The door could not disguise her laughter. "And how do you plan on doing that?"

"My father," John said, his face pressed up close to the door. "If I can send word to him, he will help. I know he will."

There was a short silence from the other side of the door. He heard footsteps retreat, then return. A goose-feather pen and paper appeared under the door. "Two guineas."

It was an exorbitant sum, but there was no use trying to bargain. He slipped the only coin he had under the door. "One now, and my father will pay another when he comes."

The woman agreed and John scratched a brief letter to his father, informing him what had happened and begging him to do whatever he could to save him from the fate of being forced to join the navy.

In the hour after he had sent the letter, John felt better. He imagined his father reading it and writing a handful of letters of his own. They would be fiercely worded and sent to influential contacts within the navy. For a while John even entertained a fantasy where a high-ranking official visited the inn personally and set him free with an apology.

His hopes died when he heard the three men outside once more and another poor victim was added to the room. The man was a drunkard who stank of urine. A miserable wretch who wouldn't last a week on board. John had nothing to say to him.

There was a small window set high up in the wall and held fast with thick bars. It offered no chance of escape, but it did allow John to mark the passing of the day as the light slowly leaked away.

It was dark outside when the last man was thrown into the room. "That's ten of you," said the head of the press-gang as the innkeeper's wife brought in a bowl of stew and jugs of water. "That's enough for one day. Enjoy your last night on land, boys."

The door had just closed when John heard a new voice outside. It was farther away from the door, but just loud enough to reach John. It was the sound of a thunderous wind tearing at the sails, the sound of anger unleashed. It was his father, and he could make out that he was commanding the man who had pressed him to release him this instant.

John could not suppress a smile as he listened. He sat back and waited for the door to open and for freedom to once more be his. Of course, his father would be livid, and John would have to repeatedly apologize for being so foolish as to be seen wearing his sailor's clothes, but that was a small price to pay.

The conversation was drowned out by the drunken man knocking over the stew and the other men shouting at him. When order was finally restored, the door opened. His father filled the frame and waited as his eyes adjusted to the darkness of the room.

"Thank you, sir," John said, standing up and trying to brush away some of the day's filth from his clothes. "I am sorry."

"No," he said. "The apology is mine. I could not secure your release. The French are threatening all along the coast and shots have been exchanged. We are not at war yet, but we will be any day. They will not release you."

John felt as if an iron manacle had been clamped over his throat. When he could speak, the words came out weak and frail. "But did you not tell them that I am about to find a merchant ship to sail with?"

Captain Newton narrowed his eyes, lowered his voice, and leaned close to his son. "If you had found a ship first and had papers to carry, they would never have taken you. But you did not take my advice, did you? You paraded around town dressed as though you were looking for a berth. You were foolish, John. Very foolish."

"What am I to do?"

"Do?" Captain Newton couldn't hide his distaste. "Your duty."

John's legs were threatening to dissolve, and he stumbled. Captain Newton reached out and gripped his arm. His hand was stronger than any iron vice.

"If you are sure that you want one day to be a captain and command men on board, you must first learn what it is to be one of them."

"But I did, sir. That last voyage. I was a common sailor, before the mast. I learned my lessons. I did."

His father's eyes burned. The grip tightened. "No. You did not. And besides, the navy is different. *War* is different. This will not be easy, John, not in the least. But I urge you to remember that this is an opportunity. You may yet emerge from this with greater prospects than you currently enjoy."

For the next several days John could still feel his father's grip on his arm. It was there as he was manacled once again and taken to the dock. He could feel it as he was rowed out to the ship, the HMS *Harwich*—a newly commissioned man-of-war with fifty guns and hundreds of sailors crammed on board. It was there as he and the other pressed men listened to the master-at-arms explain the punishment for deserting the ship, smiling as he showed them the very noose that he would use and the yardarm high up on the mast from which their lifeless bodies would hang. Most of all he felt it on his first night on board as he lay in his hammock below deck. It was darker, damper, and more crowded than any ship he had ever been on. The air was so foul and suffocating that he feared it might not be enough to sustain so many men. Panic started to rise from the deepest part of him. He lay still and remembered his father's fingers digging into his flesh. He was grateful for the distraction.

John's new life as a common sailor on board the *Harwich* was nothing like his time on the commercial ships that plied the North Sea and the Mediterranean. As a merchant sailor he was one of a crew of perhaps twenty; now he was one of three hundred. Sailing to the Mediterranean at the time had felt like a mighty challenge, but by comparison to his new posting it was a luxury. The *Harwich* patrolled the English Channel, sailing up and down under damp, gray skies. From the moment he was shaken awake, every minute was filled with shouted orders and tasks that had to be carried out double-quick. The master-at-arms watched the pressed men like a hawk and never passed on an opportunity to lash them with the thick cut of rope that he held in his hand.

The food they were given was designed to keep them meek. John was used to hardtack—biscuits made from flour and water—but not to the maggots that infested the naval stores. The salted beef and pork were as tough as old timber, and some of the sailors carved their cheese rations into buttons for their clothes.

Designed purely as an engine of war, the *Harwich* was a ship that seemed to go out of its way to deprive its own men of comfort. The hold where most of the three-hundred-strong crew slept was 5 feet high, 40 feet wide, and 140 feet long. Water crept constantly through the sides, pooling at their feet. There were rats and lice and the nauseating smell of foul bilgewater rising from the hold like an inescapable miasma. When one man went down with dysentery, it spread fast. When fights broke out, they spread even faster. Between the hours he spent working frantically on deck, where the lash of the whip was inevitable, and the hours he spent below, where violence and sickness were equally unavoidable, John's first weeks were a torture unlike any he had ever encountered. He was crushed, day after day, and treated no better than a farm horse or a slave.

One month after he was snatched from the street and taken on board the *Harwich*, John was summoned to see Captain Carteret. He had never stepped inside the captain's cabin before, had barely been in his presence for that matter. So to be escorted in by the master-at-arms, addressed by name and told to stand at attention, was almost too much to endure. If it hadn't been for the last month—and all the lessons it had taught him about living in a state of constant vigilance—he might well have collapsed right there on the floor.

"Newton," said Captain Carteret, glancing up before locking his eyes on a letter on his desk. "I have received word from Admiral Medley. It seems your father has written to him on your behalf."

The light from the oil lamp was dim, and the captain's brow furrowed as he studied the paper. John was no wiser as to why he had been summoned. He risked a glance at the master-at-arms, but his face was etched in stone.

"Yes," said the captain vaguely as he finally put the letter down. He sat back, carefully locked his fingers together in front of him, and looked up at John. "I know your father. He was a fine captain and now an agent for the Royal African Company, I hear. I have been asked to help. And I am happy to oblige."

The fear within John thawed instantly. His thoughts turned to Polly and what he might say upon their reunion. It would be hard to explain much of the previous month.

"Yes," said the captain, his eyes drawn back to the letter. "Your father has asked you be promoted to midshipman. He says you have ambitions for a career at sea, and I agree that this is an excellent opportunity for you. Serve well and you shall not make either your father or I regret it."

John muttered his thanks and was led out of the cabin and back down to the pit in which he had been locked up for weeks. At first, he felt a certain frustration and disappointment that he could not be released from the navy altogether. But as the master-at-arms directed him to gather his sea chest and bring it up to the quarterdeck and showed him the new light-filled cabin that he would be sharing with just a handful of other sailors of his rank, John's mood improved. Compared to the forecastle, it was as airy and spacious as a country house.

Almost immediately it became clear that life as a midshipman was in every way better than life as a common sailor. There were no maggots in the hardtack—and no hardtack at all for that matter—but fresh eggs from the chickens that were kept on deck. There was no master-at-arms watching over him with a rope whip in his hand, and no need to lie in his hammock fearing when the next fight would break out. Instead of being constantly full of torment, the life of a junior officer was easy.

John's new cabinmates were a mixed bunch. Some were old sea dogs in their late thirties who had progressed as high as they ever would; others were almost as young as John and full of ambition. What held them together was their disdain for lesser mortals. They saw themselves as educated, enlightened, socially superior men.

Despite being the lowest rank of officer, midshipmen considered themselves a world away from the ignorant wretches cooped down below. Up on the quarterdeck there was not a man among them who did not relish the opportunity to vent his disdain for the common sailor—especially the criminals and no-hopers who had been press-ganged from the streets or sent straight from the jails.

John kept his own story quiet, though he suspected his cabinmates knew that he had not boarded the *Harwich* willingly. To overcome any doubts they might have about him, John threw himself in with them. He carried himself as they did, walking around deck the way he had seen his father patrol a ship from stem to stern as a captain. He took every opportunity to abuse the very men he had previously served alongside, making up witty songs about the weakest, most repulsive of the wretches, and inventing new insults for those he hated the most. He gleefully picked out the men he had feared the most and ordered them to take on some humiliating, dangerous, or thankless task. He wore arrogance like a shield and used mockery as a whip. For John, becoming an officer was as easy and as natural as taking over the family business. All that was required was for him to look upon his past—the month below deck—and turn from it in shame. All that could now be erased.

It wasn't only John's initial disgrace on board that he chose to forget. The rest of the midshipmen were self-declared freethinkers—part of a growing number of fashionable elites in the eighteenth century who saw no need for faith. Thus far, John had met these ideas only in books. But here were real-life examples of the principles he embraced. His companions were an irreligious bunch, dedicated to living as if there were no God, morally independent and making their own way in life. They convinced John that he had merely toyed with the whole freethinking scheme thus far. If he really understood how revolutionary this philosophy was, he could forget Christianity altogether and throw off any remaining restraints of conscience. John found it surprisingly easy to forget the years when he willingly professed his Christian faith and had tried to live up to its demands. He was soon mocking Christianity with the best of them. He made it his business to pour scorn now on anyone who took the Bible at all seriously. His behavior soon matched his principles too. He was a "libertine" and he was "licentious"—different ways of saying: no restraints anymore for me.

When war was eventually declared in the spring of 1744, soon after John's promotion, it bore little resemblance to the dark fantasies that gripped so many people in England. For those on board the *Harwich*, at least, war changed little. They had one encounter with a French ship in which shots were fired, but every other day was made up of the same tedious journeys, escorting merchant vessels up and down the English Channel. On rare occasions they sailed as far north as Norway, but much of the time in the North Sea they turned back at Scotland.

Neither being at war nor being press-ganged into the navy had done anything to dent John's aspiration to become master of his own ship one day. He was still just as ambitious as he had been when he first shared his hopes with his father, but his time on the *Harwich* had given him a dose of reality. Life in the navy was different to life on board a merchant vessel. It was more brutal, more cramped, and much more boring. With the grunts below deck to do the hard work, John became sullen, lazy, and prone to apply the absolute minimum of effort to any task he was given, just like every other man in his cabin.

That tedium was shattered the day that Captain Carteret announced they would be resting at single anchor off the coast just north of Dover and that the men would be given twenty-four hours shore leave. The whole ship was united with delight. Men talked about taverns they would visit and whorehouses of which they had heard. John kept his plans quiet, first, because he had told nobody about his affections for Polly and, second, because he knew that any visit to her would have serious consequences for him back on the ship. The journey from the coast to Chatham would take a whole day of hard riding, but John had no intention of turning around and returning to the *Harwich* as soon as he arrived.

When he finally arrived at Chatham, John stabled the horse he had rented and strode to the Catletts' front door, home again. Or at least, so it felt to him.

It was good to see them again. It was December, and nothing much had changed in the year since he had last visited. He still felt tongue-tied and nervous whenever Polly walked in the room, and young master George still looked at him with eyes wide with fascination. In fact, he was even more delighted than ever to hear John's stories from the sea, and John dutifully supplied a stream of accounts of fierce battles against French warships.

As John fell asleep that night in master John's bedroom, he thought again about Polly. Unlike the dull ache of love that had kept him awake the first time he ever saw her, this time it was the cold stab of fear that set his heart racing. Polly was fifteen now and had grown significantly since he last saw her. She was almost a woman, and if he did not move quickly, she would surely be taken from him by some other man. As the night inched by, John decided that he would have to stay even longer at Chatham, no matter how serious the consequences. It was the third time that he could not tear himself away from the Catlett family, no matter the costs.

The next day he tried his best to impress not just young George but Polly and her parents. He kept the battle stories brief and made no mention of being pressed but talked up his promotion to midshipman. He described the increased pay, the improved conditions, and the gulf in status between his fellow officers and the common sailors beneath them.

"In short, sir," he said to Uncle George as they both warmed themselves by the fire while breakfast was being prepared, "I have prospects. I shall continue to do my duty as a naval officer, and I believe that I shall prosper. Who knows, I may be promoted any day now. And when we have won this war and sent the French ships to their graves, I may wish to leave the navy and become a merchant seaman like my father. Did you know that he has been appointed an agent with the Royal African Company? It is quite the honor for him and quite the opportunity for me."

John ran out of words and stared at the fire. A heavy silence filled the room.

After several days of telling the Catletts how impressive a suitor he was, John could wait no longer. He asked to see Polly's parents in private after supper and announced that he would be returning to the *Harwich* in the morning. He had stayed through the Christmas season and it would be New Year's Day when he rejoined his crewmates. One day's leave had turned into ten days.

"When I am away next, I should like permission to correspond directly with Polly," he said. "Your child is . . ." he paused, struggling to find the right words. He had in fact already written to Polly at her boarding school, confiding in her his own tormented feelings. He recalled writing in one of his letters: "If my loving you was a fault, I have been my own punishment."

"She is *not* a child," said Uncle George, a false smile etched on his face. "And nor are you a viable suitor. I have listened to you these last few days and heard nothing that would make me believe you are capable of making a serious proposal. So no, John, you may not write to my daughter. I forbid it."

He swept out of the room, leaving John pale and numb. He looked to Aunt Elizabeth for reassurance, but her smile was pained.

"My husband is right, John. You must give up this foolish idea. It is an impossibility. Surely you can see that?"

John could feel the anger rise but held himself in check. "I can see that I am already an officer and not yet twenty years old. I can see that I have an income and prospects. I can see that I come from a family that bears a great name within the trade. How can you say that our match is an impossibility?"

"My dear John," she said, frowning. "Do you not see that the problem is not so much your prospects? It is your father. Does he give his consent? Without it there is no hope at all of your ever marrying Polly. You can see that, surely? Either secure his permission or give up on Polly."

John stumbled from the house the next morning, barely pausing to say fare-well. He rode hard all day, taking the worst of his anger out on the horse. He was humiliated and enraged, rejected by the one family he thought cared about him. He wanted nothing more than to take Polly away from them and marry her regardless. Sooner or later, when he had made a success of himself, they would be forced to change their minds.

His mood broke the moment he saw the ship. The skies were heavy, and the ship looked starker and more foreboding than he remembered it. He had been away more than a week, and his actions would not go unpunished. He stood on the shore and called to the watch to send a boat to row him back, wondering how lucky he would be. Perhaps he might lose a month's pay. Perhaps he might be flogged. Either way, he did not care much anymore, for as he waited, he could finally see his circumstances more clearly.

The *Harwich* was useless to him. It was a floating prison, and one that was keeping him from progress and from happiness. With his father's influ-ence limited, it would take him years to advance from midshipman. What he needed was to take advantage of his father's position and find a way to leave the navy and become an employee of the Royal African Company instead. It was the only way that he could demonstrate to his father that he was worthy of his name, persuade him to lend his support to his proposal to Polly, and prove to the Catletts once and for all that the match was desirable.

By the time he was shown into Captain Carteret's cabin and told to give account of himself, he had lost all fear of punishment or consequence. The *Harwich* offered him nothing. The sooner he left, the better.

"It was for love," he announced, struggling a little to keep his footing as the ship rose and fell with the waves. "Her name is Polly and I have loved her from the very moment I first met her two years past."

The captain smiled, throwing John a little off guard. "Continue," he said, his hand waving vaguely in John's direction.

It was a long story, and John told it as best he could. He built to a cre-scendo where he described his determination to one day win Polly's hand. The whole tale was embellished here and there with as much creativity and flair as he had used to keep young George Catlett so engaged. Judging by the smile on Captain Carteret's face, John thought the result was equally impressive.

"Well, I shall allow it this time, but be warned. I shall not be so lenient the next."

John mumbled his thanks and prepared to leave.

"Tell me one last thing," the captain added.

"Sir?"

"You have been forbidden from writing to this girl. How do you plan on winning her hand?"

"I shall write to her, of course. Without delay."

Captain Carteret frowned. "You think that wise, with her parents so expressly against it? Perhaps a period of reflection would be beneficial."

"No," John said, louder than was necessary for the small room and the company within it. "'Never deliberate.' That is the motto I choose to live by. Never deliberate at all."

Thick, bruised clouds had been hovering over the *Harwich* when John boarded it. Over the following days the winter skies remained dark and foreboding. John ignored the conversation among his fellow officers of a coming storm, as well as their idle gossip about a possible new task for the *Harwich*, one which would see them venture out of their familiar territory of the English Channel and North Sea.

John weighed his words carefully and wrote to Polly one night. It was 1:00 a.m. and he had just finished a four-hour watch, but his thoughts were anywhere but on the *Harwich*.

> *The first day I saw you I began to love you. The thoughts of one day meriting you (and believe nothing less could have done it) roused me from a dull insensible melancholy I had contracted and pushed me into the world.*

Even though her mother had expressly forbidden either of them from writing to each other, he begged Polly to write back. He mailed the letter to one of

Polly's aunts—a kind woman who he hoped would be willing to play the role of cupid in this forbidden love.

He was nineteen years old, but he strove to write in a high style, equal to his feelings.

I believe a much better Pen than mine would fail in describing suitably all the tender Emotions, and pleasing inquietudes, of a heart actuated by so sincere, and strong a Passion as mine.

And he explained how determined he was to make something of his life for her sake.

I hope to succeed; but I take Love to witness, it is not wholly on my own account; for I shall not value Riches but for the opportunity of laying them at your feet.

Writing by the light of a gently swaying lantern, trimmed low, and with his sloped wooden writing box open on his lap, John dipped his pen one last time and concluded.

It is not in the power of words to express with how great ardency I am, your most devoted and faithful admirer, J. Newton.

There were other letters, and darker skies, and the endless rumors that increasingly ran through the crew like rats in the hold. The whole ship appeared to be obsessed with what lay in store for the *Harwich*, yet John couldn't summon the enthusiasm to care—not even when the ship weighed anchor off the coast of Kent and moved farther along the south coast to join a large fleet of navy and merchant vessels, all waiting for instructions.

At least, John didn't care until the day the captain announced that the rumors were true. The *Harwich* was to leave the east coast of England and escort a fleet of merchant ships heading south, rounding the Cape of Good Hope and continuing on to the East Indies where the *Harwich* would remain to protect British interests in the area.

All told, they would be away for five years.

The news hit John hard. He was right back where he started when he first met Polly—worse, even. At least five years working on a sugar plantation in Jamaica would have transformed him into a wealthy man. Five more years on the *Harwich* and he would certainly end up broke, likely so debilitated from the poor conditions on board that he would barely be able to work again, and maybe even dead.

Before John could think of a plan to secure his own transfer off the *Harwich*, a vicious storm, brewing for days, finally struck. It was as violent and brutal as any he had ever experienced. Savage winds and terrifying waves attacked the fleet at anchor. Hour upon hour it lasted, with John and the rest of the crew frantically doing all they could to keep the *Harwich* afloat and prevent it being driven into the rocks along the Cornish coast. Above the sound of wind and rain as it lashed the timbers of the *Harwich*, the only other sounds they could hear were the noise of masts breaking on ships nearby, vessels colliding, and the occasional cries of men jumping for their lives as their ships capsized.

Daylight finally brought the storm to the end. Amazingly, the *Harwich* had escaped with only minimal damage, but much of the rest of the fleet—including a number of ships flying the flag of the Royal African Company—was in a desperate condition. Those lucky enough to survive would need weeks of repairs before they could take to sea again.

And so, with the *Harwich* laid up just outside Plymouth while the rest of the fleet underwent repairs in the docks nearby, John began to form an idea. When he heard that his father would be making an inspection of the repairs to the Royal African Company's ships at nearby Torbay—just a day and a half's walk along the coast from Plymouth—the idea became a plan. All he needed was a means of getting off the *Harwich* and making it to shore. And as a midshipman whose duties included taking on supplies of fresh fruit and vegetables for the coming journey to the East Indies, it did not take long before the perfect opportunity arose.

"A word with you, Officer Newton," said Captain Carteret one morning as John prepared to climb into the longboat and row with eleven sailors to the shore to buy supplies. The captain looked concerned and kept his voice low as he spoke. "Do not let any man out of your sight, you hear me?"

Within less than an hour of telling the captain that he would obey his order, John was silently repeating his mantra, *Never deliberate.* He had slipped out of sight of the eleven crew members once on shore and was already heading out of Plymouth. He had no map, no clothes other than his standard navy issue attire, and no intention of asking anyone for directions for fear of giving himself away as a deserter. He strode east, knowing that as long as he took the coastal road he would eventually hit Torbay.

All night he walked, only pausing to rest when the thick cloud obscured the moon and made it impossible to see. The next morning, as the darkness finally receded, he took up his steady march again.

He walked through the dawn, into the fresh April morning. He ignored the pains of hunger and thirst and thought only of the future that lay ahead as an employee of the Royal African Company. He would join the hundreds of vessels that sailed from England to the Guinea coast of West Africa, west across the Atlantic to the Caribbean and the Americas beyond, before riding the trade winds back home. He would join the ranks of those making a healthy profit as they supplied the slave labor that fueled the surge in trades like sugar, cotton, and tobacco. It would be a good life, one of which he was sure the Catletts would approve.

Late in the morning John could see Torbay in the distance. Plymouth was far enough away to risk asking directions, and a farmer told him that he had just two hours left to walk. John felt himself relax just a little. If he was lucky, he would be able to find his father before dark. Maybe even meet a captain or two and see what kind of terms might be on offer.

John didn't hear the handful of soldiers. He didn't see them, either. Not until it was too late. By the time he found his voice and tried to convince them that he was not a deserter but a simple merchant sailor on the way to meet his father, the irons were already clamped tight on his wrists. The manacles bit into his skin and his back was turned on Torbay. It was like he was being press-ganged all over again.

Nobody spoke as they marched back along the country road.

By the time they entered the town itself, the silence had vanished, replaced by the jeers of onlookers. In a naval town like Plymouth, everybody knew what it meant when a man dressed as a sailor was escorted in chains by soldiers. There was a special type of contempt reserved for deserters. The shouts and insults and taunts about what punishment awaited grew louder with every step.

For two days John was held in a jail cell down by the dock. The chains never stopped biting into his flesh, just as the humiliation and sense of shame gnawed deep within. Neither of those emotions could block out the even greater fear of what would happen next. It dominated his thoughts. He might be keelhauled—bound at the wrists and ankles and dragged by rope all the way under the ship. But only if he was lucky.

Running the gauntlet was worse, with each crew member lining up to strike him as he walked the perimeter of the ship. Some men might not hit so hard, but there were others who would relish the chance to strike him.

Being flogged with a cat-o'-nine-tails was even worse yet, especially if he was flogged around the fleet—being sent to each ship at anchor for a whipping. If that happened, he'd be lucky to survive. Or unlucky, for that matter, as he'd be not only maimed but demoted to the lowest rank and trapped on board for the next five years.

Or they could just do what they usually did with deserters and swing out the yardarm at the side of the ship, hang him from the noose, and kill him quickly.

Perhaps that would be best of all.

By the time John was taken back on board the *Harwich* and finally stood face-to-face with Captain Carteret, in front of the entire crew that was assembled on deck, he was exhausted from fear and lack of sleep. He could barely listen as the captain spoke, but he could see the master-at-arms holding the cat-o'-nine-tails loosely at his side. He heard the captain describe himself as "a humane man who behaves very well to the ship's company." For the briefest of moments John wondered whether he was about to receive another reprieve, just like the time he returned late from seeing Polly.

He had no such luck.

"Master-at-arms," the captain shouted, his voice fighting against the wind. "Strip him . . . Bind him fast to the grate there . . . Now give him the first dozen . . . And the next dozen . . . And the rest."

John was barely conscious when he was taken to the surgeon's quarters. He had no idea whether his wounds were cauterized with vinegar, liquor, salt water, or hot tar. By then the pain was so great that it was impossible to think even a single coherent thought. All he knew was the agony that was tearing through every nerve, every muscle, every organ of his body.

For two days he lay facedown in the surgeon's cabin. At times he slept, but mostly he lay and tried to control the pain that ran wild like panic throughout his body.

On the third day, the surgeon declared him fit and he went back to his duties. Only, John did not return to the duties or quarters of a midshipman. He was stripped of his rank and sent back in the dark, dank hold with the rats and disease and the common sailors that he had previously treated with such contempt. From the moment he eased himself down into his hammock, trying to hide the pain as the wounds on his back opened up again, one thing was clear: he was theirs now. The captain had handed out his punishment. Now the common sailors would administer their own justice. And unlike the lashes given by the master-at-arms, it would not be over in a few minutes. For as long as he was among them, he was theirs.

Not an hour of a day went by in which John was not humiliated in some way. He tried to ignore it, to block out the taunts and the abuse just like he had when he was marched through the streets of Plymouth, but it was different this time. He was trapped. There was no escape. All he knew—and all he was ever going to know from this point on—was pain.

Five weeks after first anchoring off Plymouth in the wake of the storm, less than a week after John had been paraded on deck in front of the entire crew, the *Harwich* raised its sails and joined the fleet of merchant and navy warships that were headed south.

John was in the middle of a watch, cleaning the deck. He took a moment to pause as he stood on deck. He wasn't supposed to stop, but his wounds had opened up again and he was unable to do anything at speed. He planted his feet against the deck, as it rose and fell as the ship cut through the waves, and watched the coast of England slip from view.

The hope of a career with his father's company was lost.

The prospect of escape from the *Harwich* was gone.

The dream of a life with Polly was dead.

He looked over the gunnel to the sea below. He could jump, perhaps. That at least would offer him a way out.

Something caught his attention out of the corner of his eye, high up in the rigging. It was another sailor, a midshipman with whom he used to share a cabin. He was staring at John now, with a look stretched tight across his face that John recognized immediately. It was a look of pure contempt, a look that John had worn so many times as he strode about the ship as an officer.

"You son of a whore, Newton! You're not an officer now. Get back to work or I'll whip you myself! Captain would be pleased with me, too, I reckon."

The humiliation was more than just another wound to add to the collection. It went far deeper than the gashes torn in his back by the cat or the threats and taunts whispered in the darkness as he tried to sleep. His flesh would mend in time, but he feared his pride was broken forever.

He struggled back to work but kept an eye on the waves that churned below.

The waves would take him, that was true. Death would be quick, just a matter of a minute or two for a man like him who could not swim. But what would it achieve?

There was a better way of escaping. Something that would offer him some degree of revenge on the man who was behind all of his miseries, as well as securing his own final release.

If he killed the captain, they'd have to kill him too.

John Newton lay in his hammock and tried to lose himself in the darkness. He brooded over only two things—despair and revenge. He worked hard to ignore everything around him. The hot, lifeless air that filled the hold like poison. The shouts and busyness of life on deck. The scabs on his back that were just now tearing away from the paper-thin skin beneath. The fear that his opportunity to kill Captain Carteret might never come, or that when it did, he would be too weak and too slow to do it. John blocked it all out. All he wanted was darkness.

Outside it was probably a beautiful day. It had taken them eighteen days to reach the island of Madeira. Now, after weeks being docked in Funchal with the rest of the fleet, they had finally taken on enough provisions and prepared the ship for the long voyage east. It was their last day on the island, and many of the crew had gone on shore to celebrate. Even though it was the farthest south John had ever been, he had no interest in going ashore. If none of the men would talk with him when they were on board, they would never invite him to sit alongside them in some tavern while they got drunk and admired the whores.

So John had remained on board, trying to ignore whatever was going on above deck and disappear.

He was drifting somewhere between awake and asleep when one of his old midshipmen companions entered the hold and shouted at him to get up. "We leave for the Cape tomorrow, Newton. There's work to do, especially for a dog like you."

John kept his eyes closed and his breathing slow as he tried to feign sleep. It didn't fool the officer, who picked his way over to John, pulled his dirk from his belt, and used the long-bladed dagger to slice through the ropes that held John's hammock up.

"On deck," he growled as John collapsed in agony onto the damp timbers below. "Now."

When he finally emerged, blinking in the bright sunlight, John saw a merchant ship called the *Levant* laid up nearby. A small boat was rowing from it toward the *Harwich*, with three men on board. One of his fellow shipmates from the forecastle was standing on deck, his sea chest at his feet, tracking the rower's progress.

"Who are they?" John asked.

"Gunners," said the sailor. "Captain requisitioned them from that Guinea slaver. Says he needs them before sailing for the Cape. Traded me in their place."

"You are leaving the *Harwich*?"

The man smiled. "I'll be home within the year."

It was all that John needed to hear. He ran and found the master-at-arms, begging him to petition the captain for permission to leave the *Harwich* and transfer to the *Levant*. Captain Carteret only needed a moment or two to consider the request that this notorious troublemaker was making of him.

Within twenty minutes of being cut down from his hammock, John was climbing down the ladder toward the longboat below. He carried only the clothes on his back, a book of mathematics that he had bought back in England, and some writing tools. There had been no time to bring his sea chest or the rest of his possessions, but it did not trouble him. As he reached the end of the ladder and placed one foot on the boat, he felt an emotion he had long since forgotten—joy. The joy of freedom.

This was a new start. He was about to turn twenty years old and finally he was able to step away from the horrors of the navy. A stride forward into a new world of possibility and hope. Finally, after what seemed like years of being enslaved, he was free.

"Such a coincidence indeed," said the smiling Captain James Phelps of the *Levant*, repeating himself for the third time in less than ten minutes. His fat sausage fingers folded over his belly as he chucked to himself, finding endless amusement in the random connection being played out before him. "To think that the son of Captain Newton, with whom I am well acquainted, should find himself aboard my ship when we are so very far from home. It is a coincidence unlike any I have ever heard! I shall make special mention of it in my diary today. Mark my words!"

John returned the smile and felt himself relax. He had been on board for less than a half hour, but already it was clear that life on board the *Levant* bore practically no resemblance to his previously miserable existence on the *Harwich*. The ship was smaller, the crew smaller yet, and as far as he could tell, not one of them was forced to sleep down in the hold. The *Levant* was a slaver, but with no slaves on board it felt more like a pleasure craft. The same was true of Captain Phelps. Having been bred to the sea and grown up in the company of his father, John knew what to expect from a captain. Every single one that he had met had some variation of the same haughty air, stern rebukes, and desire to rule through fear. But Captain Phelps was different. John doubted whether he had ever so much as scolded a sailor, let alone ordered one whipped. And the captain seemed to have taken a liking to John. He made him ship steward, in charge of the stores, a position like that of surgeon, that would keep him close by the captain's side.

"Ah, Evans," said Phelps as a man not much older than John entered his cabin. "I want you to meet our latest crewmember, Mr. John Newton. Would you believe that I know this man's father? Newton, this is Mr. Evans, a Guinea trader and part owner of the *Levant*."

Evans seemed half the size of the captain but had some of the same easy air. He shook John's hand as if he were a business acquaintance and asked him pleasantly how long he had served on the *Harwich*.

"A little more than a year," John said, bracing himself for what he was sure were the inevitable questions to follow. None came. Neither Evans nor the captain appeared to be the least bit interested to find out how he landed on the *Harwich* or why Captain Carteret was so willing to let him go. As far as they were concerned, the only aspect of John's past that was remotely interesting was his father.

John exhaled a little more of the tension that he had lived with for so long.

The conversation quickly turned to the *Levant* and both men were keen to ask whether John had ever served on a Guinea slaver before.

"No," said John, before hastily adding, "sir," not really sure if it was required. "Though my father is an employee of the Royal African Company."

"Well, I never!" chimed Captain Phelps as he slapped his hand on his thigh and beamed at Evans. "Nothing but coincidences, I tell you. So, Newton, there is little need for me to tell you how this business works. You know how we bring iron bars, cloth, and arms from England and use them to barter for slaves as we travel up and down the Guinea coast. It takes a devil of a long time, I tell you. But we are lucky to have a man of Mr. Evans's skill and experience with us. Thanks to him we can fill the hull with blacks until it's fit to burst, then head west across the Middle Passage to the West Indies. Once there we sell em', fill up with sugar and rum, then hurry back on the trade winds home to England. A sailor like you can make a fair wage if you last out the fevers. Who knows, if you develop a taste for the life, you might even make your fortune like Evans here. He's building a factory right on the Guinea coast."

"A factory?" John had never heard the word used by Guinea traders before.

"Not so much a factory," said Evans. "Think of it more like a trading post or a market. You might even call it a warehouse or holding pen. These blacks are like animals out in the wild. Just as a skilled poacher gathers pheasants or deer or boar out in the countryside before traveling to market to sell, so local traders pick up blacks inland and bring them to the coast for sale. Whether the slaves brought here first became captives as prisoners of some infernal African war, or through kidnapping, or just by getting on the wrong side of the law like a criminal back home—it doesn't much matter to us. No matter how far inland it all begins, even hundreds of miles, they get passed along eventually to our factories and put up for sale. Only, while every town in England has its market square, there are too few factories along the Guinea coast to keep up with demand. Ships like the *Levant* spend months traveling up and down the coast, buying only one or two blacks at a time. With my factory, I intend to supply as many as possible, reducing the amount of time spent along the coast for Guineamen and increasing their profits. I have in mind a small offshore island, protected on all sides by the sea and with easy access to European ships."

"You see," the captain said, beaming. "Evans here is as shrewd a business-man as you will ever meet. Why, not five years ago, when he was little more than your age now, I should wager, Evans was as poor as a church mouse. Look at him now! A quarter share in a Guinea trader, a factory on the way, and even a black wife waiting for him on the coast. This is a fine business, I tell you. A fine business, and a fine life for a man like you. Yes, I think you shall like the *Levant* very much. Very much indeed."

Evans nodded in agreement and smiled at John.

For the first time in weeks, John realized that he could not feel any pain in his back.

Over the coming days, John was more and more inclined to agree with his captain's assessment. The mood among the crew was peaceful and calm. The tasks for each watch were awarded fairly, and there was no sign of a master-at-arms or bosun standing over the crew with a suspicious eye and a ready whip. With no evidence of any rats on board, even the ship's cats appeared to be superior to those on board the *Harwich*—all of which had died not long after leaving Plymouth.

Despite the fact that trading was yet to begin, the *Levant* was not, however, quiet. From the first traces of daylight until the dying rays of the sun disappeared, the ship was a cacophony of sawing, banging, and swearing as the carpenter directed his men in their work. Having picked up supplies of timber in Madeira, the race was on to prepare the ship for trading.

The changes required were extensive, particularly in the hold. The space needed to be divided horizontally by platforms, doubling the carrying capacity of the ship. It was cramped work for the carpenter and his men, crouching down with little more than two feet of clearance above them, but John was impressed by the way they kept at their work.

The ship quickly transformed before his eyes. Leaving Funchal it had felt like a pleasure cruiser. By the time they neared the coast, it looked more like a floating prison. Vertical barriers needed to be erected throughout the hold to separate slaves. The biggest change of all was on deck, where a thick, ten-foot-tall fence known by the crew as the *barricado* was created. It ran right across the deck, even protruding beyond it. There were pikes and guns mounted on top, and the day it was finished everyone cheered with relief.

"Guinea slavers need special preparation," said Evans as John stared at the thick nets that were being strung along the side of the gunnel, all around the deck. "The blacks would sooner die than sail. The nets are essential."

"And the barricado?"

Evans frowned. "The women and children are safe enough, so we keep them on this side. But the men are savages and will fight for their lives. Give them even the slightest opportunity and they'll try to kill every last one of us."

"I had no idea that it was so . . ." said John, his voice trailing off.

"Dangerous? Not many people do. And it is even more so on the coast. There are swamps that will swallow you, fevers that will kill you in a day, and an endless succession of tribal wars that no European man could hope to walk away from. Even the witchcraft and superstitions that they follow appear to have power. Any man who sets foot upon African soil is placing himself at risk. Even if you stay on the ship, you can be killed—not just by the blacks on the other side of the barricado either. I have seen many a good sailor lose his life here to wine, to weather, or to women."

He stopped and looked at John. He smiled.

"But there's gold there, too, *black* gold," said the captain, twirling a glittering gold coin between his fingers. "That is why we call this bit of money a guinea after all. For the man who is brave enough to leave the ship and step ashore, there are fortunes to be made."

John's strength quickly returned, and so, too, did his confidence. Before the week was out, he had forgotten what it had felt like to be the miserable wretch on the *Harwich*, demoted to the rank of common sailor, despised by all. Among the crew of the *Levant* he could hold his head high as steward, and he soon remembered what it felt like when he was a midshipman. Spending time in the company of men who treated him well, he felt no need to hide himself away when his watch was over. He could be himself again. He was free. Free from the shackles of being known. Free to reinvent himself as a young man, giving full vent to his passions with little care for propriety.

That freedom found its voice one night soon after arriving on the *Levant*. The crew had worked hard all day, and the barricado was well on the way to completion. They gathered around the cooking pot on deck and opened a fresh gallon of rum. The whole crew sat happily, united and filling the night sky with the sound of their singing.

John knew many of the old shanties they were singing, but as the rum flowed and their voices grew hoarse from laughter, a few of the men tried making up their own rhymes. They were a mixed bag—some so poor as to be laughable, most just plain strange—but when it was John's turn to lead, he discovered that the words came to him as fast as sailors gather round an open cask of rum.

He sang about the barricado, keeping the savages at bay.

He sang about the ship, the seaborne prison that would carry them all to riches.

And then he discovered his muse. Captain Phelps. Fattened up like a prize pig and constantly sputtering on about some nonsense or other, the captain was a lyricist's dream. With just a handful of rhyming couplets, John had the whole crew in stitches.

Although the captain didn't say anything at first, there was an icy chill that settled in between them. He simply listened for a while, then turned on his heel, muttered something under his breath, and instructed the first mate, William Miller, that he required his presence in his cabin to plan the next day's tasks. John had lost his favor and made yet another enemy.

There was no laughter on the morning when the *Levant* finally caught sight of the coast of West Africa. The crew stood transfixed. Nobody spoke. The air itself was spiked with fear.

It was Captain Phelps who broke the silence. "Look there," he said, pointing to a thin plume of smoke rising in the sky a mile or two south. "They are ready to trade. Think not of the dangers, men. Think of the profits."

The crew returned to work and brought the *Levant* as close as they dared to the coast. The sound of the waves breaking on the shore was almost as loud as a storm, and John pitied Evans and the rest of the poor men whose job it was to try to row the smaller trading vessel from the *Levant* to shore. The breakers started at least one hundred feet from shore, and sharp rocks littered the coast for miles around. More than once the traders came perilously close to capsizing. For a while John had to turn away, and he only looked up when the crew's cheering told him that the traders had finally been able to land.

There was much to do while they were gone, and John was given the task of checking the stores and ensuring that the hold was ready. Stray nails, misplaced tools, even a thick splinter of wood could become a weapon in the hands of someone desperate enough to escape the *Levant*. The headroom was minimal, yet John was just about able to crawl around on his hands and knees as he checked.

He returned to the deck, his back and limbs more than a little sore, to find the first mate making his own preparations. Miller was sorting through a sea chest full of thumb screws, chains, shackles, and collars. After carefully checking that each one was strong and secure, he laid them out on the deck, separating those designed for children from the rest. He returned John's stare with a knowing smile.

It took almost the entire day before the shout went up that the traders were returning. John had finished his watch and stared as the men struggled against the waves. He tried to make out how successful Evans's trading had been, but it wasn't until they finally tethered up against the *Levant* and hauled their catch on board that John could see what they had brought with them. Two men and one woman. They were all naked. The woman was staring at the cooking pot, shaking. At least four of the crew had taken up small arms and had them trained on the newcomers.

"My word!" said Captain Phelps as Evans stood on deck, wiping the salt spray from his face. "This is a very good start indeed." The captain nodded to the first mate who grabbed each slave in turn, first prizing open their jaws to examine their teeth, then slapping, pinching, and prodding the rest of them. "Not too tall, not too small. No ugly faces. Her breasts are not long and tripeish. They all have their fingers and toes and most have their teeth. My word! You really do know how to get the very best blacks available, Mr. Evans. Very well done, sir!"

As the captain quizzed Evans about the price he had paid, Miller chained them together and led them through the barricado down into the hold below.

"Three down," chimed the captain as they disappeared from view. "Only 497 left to go!"

For the next six months life continued much as it had on that first day of trading. The *Levant* sailed along the coast, sometimes for days on end as it searched for larger factories or the smoke signs of small-scale traders. When they found one, they would drop anchor and wait while Evans or Miller went trading. Sometimes they were gone for hours, sometimes for days. Sometimes they returned to the ship with nothing, sometimes with as many as six or seven slaves. The barricado was constantly manned by armed guards, and routine checks of the hold were carried out. It was a slow business, and with every slave put in irons and chained in pairs, the tension on board rose.

They still sang at night from time to time, and John took extra pleasure in making the men laugh with his songs. But it was different. They were no longer just sailors navigating the seas. They were jailors, prison guards constantly alert to the threat of insurrection. With every successful trade, the risks to their safety increased. Each night, the threat level climbed higher.

Death, when it eventually did come to the *Levant*, arrived in the most surprising of ways. By the time they were done trading, they had shackled more than 480 men, women, and children on board. Many of them died even before the ship was ready to leave the coast of Africa. The hold was so full that not a single night went by without the sounds of scuffling coming from below. Down there the slaves were treated like animals—the bodies crowded, chained in pairs, like some diabolical version of Noah's ark, each locked in their own claustrophobic struggle for survival.

The *Levant* was one or two trades away from being at capacity, and therefore ready to make final preparations before beginning the Middle Passage west across the Atlantic. Apart from Evans—who was intending to leave the ship when it made its final stop near the island on which he was to build his factory—the crew were desperate to leave the Guinea coast. Dozens on board had already succumbed to tropical diseases and died. Each time the captain emerged on deck and addressed them, they hoped it would be to announce their departure.

Yet one morning Captain Phelps never emerged from his cabin. It was only after First Mate Miller went inside to rouse him that they knew why. He had died in the night, apparently peacefully.

The crew were troubled, but Miller took immediate command. He announced that they would forget about any more trades and would sail as soon as they were ready for the West Indies. At first John assumed that he would continue to sail with the *Levant* all the way back to England. But when he heard it rumored that the first mate—now Captain Miller—had taken a dislike to him and intended to trade him to the first navy vessel they met, he panicked.

It was left to Evans to suggest a workable solution. He offered to take John on as an apprentice while he built his factory. There was too little time to discuss things like payment and terms, and again, just like with the *Harwich*, John found himself with a momentous decision to make about his future and barely any time in which to consider it. He was bound in service to a new master before he knew it.

"Never deliberate," he said quietly to himself as he carried his clothes and his book of mathematical theorems by Euclid and his wooden writing box and followed Evans down the ladder into a small single-masted boat. It was one that could be sailed or rowed equally well—an elegant and lightweight shallop—and they set out first to the Banana Islands and then farther south, anchoring just off the largest of the Plantain Islands at the mouth of the Sherbro River. He could see that they were about two miles from the mainland. They were some seventy miles southeast of Sierra Leone now but still in an area of intensive trading with English ships.

"There," said Evans, pointing out the low-slung strip of land that was covered in palm trees and could not have been more than a mile in width. "That is where we shall build the factory. And as soon as we are finished, I shall send for P. I."

"Pee eye? What's that?"

"Not what. Who. P. I. is my wife. She will be most intrigued to meet you, I can assure you of that, Newton."

When she first stepped out of the dugout canoe onto the soft sands of Plantain Island and saw the work that her husband Evans had carried out, Princess P. I. of the Bombo family—first daughter of the chief of the Bullom people who ruled the low-lying lands from Leopard Island all the way to the bay of Sherbro—narrowed her eyes and gently raised her head in satisfaction. It was exactly as she had planned it. Exactly as she had instructed him.

The island was perfectly located. It was less than an hour's journey by canoe from the mouth of the Sherbro River—far enough from the coast to be safe, close enough to be able to trade. The buildings had been constructed in the Bullom style. Only the strongest palms had been used for the walls, and the woven plantain thatch on each roof appeared to be thick and tight enough to withstand the storms that would tear at the island as the rains came. They were on the coastal side of the island and were protected from the worst of the sea winds, but also hidden from view by a thick line of trees. It was only a matter of time before news of the factory would spread and some other tribe would decide to search it out and plunder her wealth, but at least they would struggle to find it.

Beyond the fact that her husband had followed her instructions, what pleased her most was the size of the buildings themselves. They were larger than she had expected they would be. Large enough to accommodate more slaves. Large enough to generate more profits.

Trailed by her four closest servants, she approached the factory slowly, her eyes taking in every detail. Besides the barracoon—a holding pen for the slaves that would be sold to the white traders—there was a storeroom where they would keep the guns, knives, and other items used for trade. There were sleeping quarters for her own servants, a kitchen, pens for livestock, a plot for growing vegetables, and even an area where her husband had agreed one day to plant her a garden in the European style. When it was complete with its row of lime trees to walk down and a shaded area in which to sit, she would entertain the white traders there and conduct their affairs. It would be so much more pleasant than the places they usually traded—tiny huts on rocky outcrops up and down the coast. But here, with their boats at anchor safely nearby and a cool glass of freshly squeezed lime juice in their hands—not to mention the number of slaves they could supply—she could command any price she wished.

She paused outside her own sleeping quarters. They were the grandest of all—almost as big as the slave buildings but with shuttered windows on all sides to allow a cool breeze to circulate—but still no match for a princess. She turned away. Her time on the island would only be temporary.

"My lady!"

She turned back to see Evans in her sleeping quarters, tools in his hands and sweat in his hair. He looked nothing like a prince. And yet, as he approached her with his eyes dancing fire and his face painted with joy, she let her feet stay planted in the soil, felt her eyes close just a little and her head lift toward the sun. Among all the white men that her father had ever traded with, Evans was the only one she had ever liked.

He dropped his tools on the ground and came close enough to reach out and gently take her hand, bowing gracefully. After so many days apart, his touch was even more pleasing. Neither wanted to let go.

"My lady," he said softly, his face close enough for her to see the beads of sweat above his lips. "I have missed you."

She closed her eyes and bowed her head. To be reunited at last was sweeter than even the gentlest summer breeze.

When she looked up again, the spell only lasted a moment. From the corner of her eye she saw a man—another white man—violently scratching the back of his neck as he stood in the doorway to the sleeping quarters, *her* sleeping quarters.

Evans turned and motioned the man to approach. "This is Newton," he said. "He helped a good deal on the house and factory these past weeks. Newton, come and greet my good lady wife."

The man was younger than her husband and just as sweaty. He had none of her husband's manners though. For he locked his own eyes directly on her as if she were an unmarried woman. P. I.'s eyes shot back to Evans, but he was oblivious to her displeasure.

"He is your servant?"

"Newton? No. He was on the *Levant* with me. I think he can be of use. Once he learns how, he can help trade with the Europeans."

"I do not need any help with the white traders."

"No, no, of course not. But as the business grows, he will prove useful."

"He has not worked as a trader before?"

"No. He is a sailor. A good one too."

"A sailor? Is this a boat we are standing on?"

Evans laughed, but only briefly when he saw that P. I. was not.

"No. But he can learn everything we want to teach him."

"Who will teach him?"

"I will, my dear."

"When will you teach him?"

Evans moved closer. "My dear, I . . ."

His words vanished. P. I.'s feet demanded that she move, but she stayed. Evans was a good man and she trusted him. But he knew little about trading. And this Newton clearly knew even less.

"Mrs. Pee Eye," said Newton, forgetting to bow and instead holding out his hand as if he expected her to take it. "I am honored to meet you."

P. I. glared at both men. Both were smiling at her. She had no smile for them. She let the long silence grow even longer, until Evans finally understood what she was communicating.

"Newton," he said, a sting of irritation in his voice. "You go back and finish your work there. I'll show my good lady wife the fruits of our labors."

From the moment he arrived on Plantain Island, John worked harder than he had ever worked in his life. First there was the land to clear. Then there were logs to prepare and the buildings to construct. He spent days tilling the soil in the vegetable plot, planting seeds that Evans said would quickly turn into yams. Then, once P. I. arrived, the work became even more intense. He soon realized that he was more properly her servant than Evans's. Every morning she toured their corner of the island with her husband, describing new adjustments she had devised or mistakes she wanted rectified. She was a relentless perfectionist, a person with an ambitious goal and an awareness of the high standards required to reach it. She held herself with poise and confidence, and there were many times when she reminded John of his father.

Difficult as the work was, it was made infinitely harder by the conditions. In the months he had spent trading along the Guinea coast on board the *Levant*, John had experienced the heat that the region was known for. It was brutal, but at least at sea the wind could be relied upon to reduce the temperature slightly. On the island, there was none. No breeze to cool him, and no breeze to keep away the insects that feasted on him day and night. By the time P. I. arrived, John's limbs were covered in angry red welts that he could not stop scratching, despite Evans's advice to leave them well alone.

John struggled on for as long as he could, but by the time the work was complete, the physical toil, the heat, and the mosquitoes caught up with him. A little less than four weeks after his arrival on the island, on the day that he and Evans were due to board the shallop and embark on a two-month journey inland to buy slaves, John fell sick.

"This is not good," said Evans as he stood in the doorway to John's sleeping quarters—a small hut adjacent to his and P. I.'s own quarters. "You have a fever. Are you in pain?"

"A little," said John, blinking the sweat out of his eyes. "It will pass."

"Perhaps. But not quickly. You must stay here while I go and trade. I will take one of the servants. You can accompany me on the next trading excursion."

John barely put up any resistance. Talking had made the shooting pains in his head and back even worse. It was all he could do to mumble an apology and fall back onto his sleeping mat, shivering uncontrollably in the heat.

When two of P. I.'s servants visited later that day, John was feeling even worse. His vision was blurred, and he had trouble understanding what the women were trying to say to him in their broken English. Eventually they abandoned talking, rolled him from his mat, and forced him to stand and follow them. He stumbled along between them as though he was in a dream and was powerless to resist. He was grateful when the walking was finally over and they showed him into a large enclosure, fenced round with sharpened stakes. The air was cooler, and when the door closed behind them it was dark. He lay down on wooden planks—planks that he had some faint memory of cutting and laying himself—and wondered why he had been taken to the slave factory. Before long he slipped back into his fever.

He had no idea how many days and nights he lay there, though he did know there were many occasions when he cried out desperately for water. Nobody ever came.

When John's fever finally broke, he pulled himself from the floor and stumbled to the door, half expecting to find it locked. It was open, but the blinding sunlight that flooded in and sent daggers into his head was enough to make him close it again.

It took John a long time to summon the will to step outside, and even longer to get halfway toward the clearing where the sleeping quarters lay. He collapsed and once again felt strong hands lift him to his feet and take him back to the factory.

Drifting in and out of consciousness, he was aware of strangers at times offering him a little food and water. John was so desperate with hunger that he didn't care that the bowl of rice was only half full, or that the half-chewed scraps of meat had clearly been scraped from P. I.'s plate. His body would take whatever nourishment it could get. Sometimes even the slaves in chains felt sorry enough for him to share some of their meager rations with him.

The days following his malarial fever blurred one into the other. The only way to distinguish them was John's contact with the mistress and her servants. Some days the servants would bring food, some days none. On rare days they would issue an invitation for John to visit his host in her quarters. Those were the days John dreaded. The walk itself was exhausting, but the treatment when he arrived was even worse.

The first time he staggered into P. I.'s presence, she was eating. She made a point of not inviting him to sit and only offered him food once she had finished. She held out a plate of scraps—a piece of bone china that would not have looked out of place in any dining room in England—and motioned for him to approach. Hunger cramped his stomach, and his hands were trembling so much that no sooner had he taken the plate than it dropped on the ground, smashing into a dozen pieces.

P. I. stared at him.

He bent down and tried to pick up the broken plate, but his hands were shaking.

P. I. laughed.

"Go," she said. "Back to your cell."

The moon was full that night. John could not sleep, so he slipped outside and carefully made his way toward the sleeping quarters. There were no signs of life—no fire, no dogs running around—but he moved slowly, careful not to make a sound.

When he reached the vegetable plot he fell on the ground and started to dig with his hands. The yams were barely as thick as his thumb and nowhere near ready for harvest. He crammed them into his mouth all the same. The soil was bitter, but he chewed and spat and chewed until he had a mouthful of dry, fibrous yam to swallow. He kept eating, forcing another mouthful down. Then another.

He thought he heard someone stirring nearby, so he hurried back. The moment he laid down, a fresh wave of pain shot through his stomach, radiating out. It was far worse than any hunger pains. In seconds he was doubled over, a pool of vomit and feces growing ever bigger around him.

When P. I. finally did visit John in person, several days later, he was so weak that he barely lifted his head.

"Why do you not stand when your mistress enters? Are you some kind of savage with no manners?"

John struggled to his feet and saw P. I. was not alone. All her servants were with her. They were looking at him, the same blank expressions on their faces.

P. I. said something to them that John could not understand. They laughed. When he tried to get up, she motioned to her attendants to push him back down. More laughter.

"You are idle," she said. "You lie here doing nothing. Contributing nothing. Offering nothing. I think you could not even walk out of here without one of my servants to carry you. Worthless wretch! Why are you here?"

John had spent hours lying in the darkness trying to fathom why P. I. hated him so much. No answer had ever come. But here, in this empty room with everyone looking on and P. I. staring at him as though he were a wounded snake that she was tempted to kill, he knew that knowing why she felt as she did mattered little. What counted was how he responded to her challenge. If he remained lying down, she would win. And if she won now, what would she do to him next?

John struggled to his feet. He ignored the ache in his limbs, the thirst that screamed from every cell in his body, the searing pain in his head. He held his head as high as he could and walked toward his captor.

She did not move, so he walked around her and out the door. It was slow, painful progress, but he carried himself with what little bit of dignity he could summon. First one foot, then the other. The dirt clogged his toes. He stumbled a little. Heard laughter behind him. He carried on. First one foot, then the other.

Something hit him on the back of the head. It was hard and it hurt, but he did not stop to look down and see what it was. He simply walked, slow and dignified, away from them.

Only, they did not let him go alone. The servants ran after him, crowding around. They threw more things at him—limes, he realized—and pressed on ahead of him, mimicking his awkward gait.

Again he stumbled.

Again they laughed.

More limes.

More laughter.

And on and on it went.

Plantain Island, though the largest of the three islands collectively called the Plantains, was no more than two miles in circumference, but it was big enough for John to find places to hide. He spent his days as far away from the factory as he could, where the palm trees were thickest. He only ever returned when darkness fell.

Sometimes there was food waiting for him. Sometimes not. Whenever there was something to eat, he crammed it into his mouth without ever looking at it. Experience had told him that it was better not to know.

The day that Evans returned, John was watching from the safety of the trees. The sun was low in the sky, and he was about ready to return to his quarters when he saw the shallop come into view. Evans was at the helm, a broad smile on his face.

John tracked around the island, keeping Evans in sight. He watched him come into shore, secure the boat, and call for P. I. to come and see the slaves he had bought. There were eight of them. Nine if you counted the infant clinging tight to one of the women.

He watched P. I. float gracefully toward Evans. Saw him bow, then parade the slaves. She examined them carefully, taking her time with each one.

John seized his opportunity and burst out from the trees.

"Newton?" Evans took a step back. "What the devil are you doing there? You look like a ghost."

"Sir," John fumbled as his eyes flicked to P. I., his words getting stuck like a lamb caught in a bush of thorns. "Sir, I am glad to see you again. There has been some terrible misunderstanding. Your wife. She has taken great offense at something I have done, though I have no knowledge of what it might be. She has treated me very badly these last two months. I have been a prisoner, I tell you. A prisoner. Please, sir, would you help? Tell her I am a good man and have never sought to harm her."

Evans took a step back. He turned to P. I.

She finished looking at the woman slave and the baby she was holding, then turned slowly and walked to Evans's side.

"My dear Mr. Evans," she said, offering her hand. "You have bought well. I am pleased."

Evans smiled. "But Newton here. What does he mean by this?"

P. I. leaned closer. "He cannot be trusted. Every word that falls from his lips is a lie."

John had almost finished writing the letter when he heard the crack of a branch nearby. His pen froze above the page. He studied the undergrowth. This deep into the cluster of palm trees, in the monochrome light of dawn, it was hard to see anything much. It was hard to hear, too, with the constant roll of the waves on the beach.

"Who's there?" he called.

The light shifted and he saw P. I.'s servant standing at the edge of the trees.

"It's you," John said, his eyes returning to the page as he quickly wrote the last words to his father.

Two days earlier John had been working with the servant, preparing their first batch of slaves for sale. In a quiet moment when nobody else was around, the servant had shown John the leather bag in which Evans's letters were stored, ready to be taken on board whichever European ship bought the slaves, and eventually delivered once back in England. The servant had mimed John writing and him placing the letter in the bag.

It had seemed so simple at the time, but now as John folded the letter, sealed it with wax, and held it out to be taken, he paused. "You are sure this will go undetected?"

The servant frowned, confused.

"Your mistress," John tried again, a spasm of anxiety clawing at his throat. "P. I. She will not hear of this?"

The servant stared blankly. Then he took the letter and left.

Evans's return to the island had put a halt to P. I.'s open hostility and abuse. P. I. ignored him, pretending that he was invisible. Yet John was under no illusions about his status. He had been moved out from the empty factory the day the new group of slaves arrived and told to sleep near the rest of the servants, in a hut shared with the blacksmith. John spent long days working, continuing to follow P. I.'s instructions for further adjustments to the factory, as well as helping Evans manage the slaves. They needed guarding constantly, plus feeding and regular checks to make sure that they were not making plans to escape.

Soon after writing to his father—begging for help so that he, too, might escape the island and P. I.'s tyranny—John was surprised when Evans invited him to sit down and share a drink of water one afternoon.

"I shall be leaving again in a few days," he said. "Just as soon as these slaves are gone."

"Trading?" John could hear the tremor in his own voice.

"Yes. Might be gone longer this time too. I want to go farther up toward the Rio Grande, taking a branch called the Rio Nuña. It is a little far, but there are rumors of a war inland and I expect there to be an increased supply as a result."

The thought of being under P. I.'s power again for longer was enough to send John panicking.

Evans looked at him and laughed. "Fear not. I want you to accompany me."

They set off in the shallop a week later. At first all was well. The shallop was small, only twenty-six-feet long, and the cabin was barely big enough for John and Evans and the male servant that accompanied them to lie down among the various supplies packed for the voyage. But just being back in a boat made John feel at home, as if things were starting afresh.

They had clear sailing north past the mouth of the Sierra Leone River and the Bullom Shore, hugging the coastline near Cape Verga. Finally, they reached the Nuña, the southernmost estuary of the marshy Rio Grande delta, and made their way cautiously inland. They had barely been on the river for twenty-four hours, however, when the atmosphere soured.

It was morning and they were at anchor on the river, ten miles in from the coast. For the first time in almost a year John could not hear or smell or taste the sea in the air. It troubled him to sit on the bank of the river and stare at the forest all around. There was no way of seeing through the dense undergrowth, no way of knowing what was hiding within the trees. Even the air felt lifeless and threatening.

Evans was on board, making noise inside the cabin as he searched for something. "Newton!" His voice pierced the air. "Newton!"

He came out onto the deck and stared at John on shore. His face was violent red and his fists were clenched.

"Where is it?"

"Where is what?"

"The food. Some of it is missing. Where is it?"

"I have not taken anything," John stammered. "Mr. Evans, please. I have not taken anything from you."

"You are a liar and thief, Newton. You are as worthless as my wife says. I was drinking with a brother-trader I met on the river last night, and he warned me that you were stealing from me. I have been checking my goods to see what might be missing. How dare you abuse me like this!"

"I am many things," John pleaded. "I am a lecher and a blasphemer but not a liar. I have lost everything I once valued, but not my honesty. I do not lie to you."

It was no use. The more John protested, the more irate Evans became. Soon he had jumped from the shallop onto the riverbank and was pushing John in his chest. Instinct told John to run, but there was nowhere to go. The forest around him was a prison.

"Take him on board," Evans shouted to the servant. "Chain him to the deck."

There were ankle fetters on metal chains fastened securely on the deck, ready and waiting for the slaves. They were made for smaller men than John, and the metal bit hard into his ankle. He winced at the pain but said nothing.

John spent the rest of the day chained to the deck like a dog on a leash. He was there while Evans and the servant disappeared off into the forest, and he was there when they returned, hours later as the sun was setting.

He was there all night.

All through the next day as they made their way farther up the river, John remained on deck. At some point the servant brought John some rice, but that was all. Evans ignored him, as if the man sitting hunched and huddled on the deck was just another slave he had bought.

Days passed and John remained on deck. Sometimes Evans and the servant would anchor the boat and head off to trade, leaving John alone all night, tormented by the sounds of the forest as it came alive in the darkness, feasted upon by mosquitoes and other insects. John had never feared anything as much as he feared Africa.

The chain was long enough to allow him to reach the edge of the boat, but no farther. On the days when he was alone, John explored the deck. He found some rotting meat, a fishing line, and hook, and was able to catch just enough fish to sustain him.

With only a cotton shirt, trousers, a handkerchief that he used as a hat, and a length of cloth that he used as a blanket, he was exposed to the elements. There were storms as fierce as any he had ever experienced, and nights when the temperature plummeted so low that he thought he would freeze. Long days in the sun were the worst, and soon his skin blistered and cracked. His chained ankle was particularly bad, with a great sore opening up around it.

If Evans was troubled by the sight of his former apprentice in such a condition, he did not show it. The trading was going well, and the boat soon became home to others. Evans chained them up by their ankles too. John could feel their stares. He could not return them. His body was broken, and so was his spirit.

When the shallop was full—seven males and three females—Evans turned it around and returned to the coast and sailed for Plantain Island. He was smiling as they made their way south, even looking at John and calling out, "We have traded well, Newton. Very well, indeed."

John said nothing. It had been two months since anyone had called him by name, and he felt as though he had almost disappeared. He said nothing to Evans though. Even if his throat had not been parched, he doubted he could have found the words.

The closer they got to the island, the happier Evans appeared. He was practically singing as he anchored the boat in the shallows and called out to P. I. on shore. He left John on board while he unchained the slaves and paraded them to his wife, basking in her praise at such a good selection for such good proceeds.

When Evans returned to the boat, he was smiling and humming to himself as he bent down to unlock John and free him from the chain that had held him for the better part of two months. He helped John out of the boat and onto the sand.

John felt the first mists of hope return. It was faint, but for the first time in two months, there was hope. Perhaps things would be different now. He swallowed hard, trying to coax his voice back into life.

"Mr. . . . Evans," he rasped. The words were so weak they were drowned out by the waves. He tried again. "Mr. Evans, I . . . apologize for whatever harm I have done you . . ."

Evans turned to face him. He was still smiling. Then he turned back to the island and let out a mighty shout.

"Blacksmith!" His voice was loud enough to drown out the wind and the waves, loud enough for the blacksmith to come running to his side. "I need you to make a new pair of ankle fetters."

"Another pair? We have many already."

"Those are too small and do not allow for movement. I need some for John here. He needs to be able to work, but not escape."

However bad the two months had been on the shallop, life back on Plantain Island was worse. John was still chained, still fed scraps from his master's plate, and still spent his days exposed to the elements. Only now he was set to work, planting out the avenue of lime trees that P. I. had demanded. The ground was packed tight with stones, and each hole he dug felt like a grave. At the end of each backbreaking day, he returned to the shack that he had been given beside the rest of the servants and collapsed, hands raw and bleeding, exhausted. On good nights he was so tired he barely noticed the mosquitoes and black flies that swarmed around him.

The rest of the servants appeared to have been instructed to ignore the wild-eyed European man in leg chains who shuffled around the island. He was invisible to them, as if an enslaved free man was too great a paradox to comprehend. Only one man—the same servant who had offered to smuggle John's letter into Evans's mailbag—would look at John. He would even share his own food with John when nobody was looking. At first John would try to mime his thanks, but the man never responded. He only ever stared in silence, as if he thought John was too fragile to cope with an attempt at conversation.

The physical toil was great, but it was not the greatest torment he faced. Evans had placed him under the command of one of the servants, an austere man who only ever communicated to John with prods from his heavy wooden staff. He was always silent and spent most of his time staring out to sea. Whenever he did glance at John to check his progress, he only looked for the shortest possible time. John could feel his distaste.

P. I. and Evans, on the other hand, took delight in paying regular visits to check on John's progress. They would march across to the lime-tree avenue most afternoons and never missed an opportunity to laugh at him.

"And how goes the slave's progress today?" Evans chimed one day as he and P. I. stood, fanning themselves in the fast-fading sun. John's overseer shot back some remark or other in a language that was incomprehensible to John. Yet its meaning was clear and P. I. launched into her familiar refrain. "You are too slow. You are idle," she sneered. "You are a bad slave."

"No, my darling," said Evans, his voice thick as honey. "Newton here is not a slave. He is lower than that. He is the *servant* of slaves."

They both laughed long and loud.

From that day on, John's name was erased from their minds. He was never referred to as anything other than "servant of slaves." At first the humiliation stung, but the exhaustion and physical pain weighed heavier. As the months passed and John was daily reminded that his value was beneath that of the very people they were trading, he sank deeper and deeper into his own despair.

He tried to keep himself tethered to his old life, to the truth of who he was. He kept track of the date and would mark whatever anniversary he could—five months since he first arrived on Plantain Island, eleven months since he left the *Harwich*, three years and three months since he first met Polly. At first he relished the sweetness of these memories. He cherished the hours he lay awake, remembering his former life, when he was confident and self-assured and full of optimism about the life ahead of him. But soon the memories soured. The gulf between his past and present was too vast to ignore. He was trapped now. He would be the servant of slaves for the rest of his life.

"I wonder," said Evans one afternoon as he and P. I. inspected John's work.

"If by the time these trees are fully grown and bearing fruit, our young servant of slaves here might have earned for himself a promotion. He is clearly a man of great talents after all."

"He might have left us," P. I. mused, her voice tinged with fake sorrow.

"Left us and become . . ." Evans searched for a moment. "A man of business?"

"A captain!"

"Ha! A captain of his own slave ship!"

"Yes," said P. I. They were both laughing now. "And one day this great trader might sail down to our humble island and grace us with his presence. We will do business together, drink the juice of these limes, and toast his great success!"

As the torment deepened, John turned to the one item in his possession that he had brought with him—his copy of Euclid's treatise on mathematics. When his work was completed for the day, he would disappear to some corner of the island where he could not be seen. There, crouched over the sand, he would trace the ancient theorems out with a stick. "Isosceles is a triangle which hath only two sides equal . . ." There was comfort in the endless repetition.

However, even the power of Euclid to distract or offer refuge waned in time.

It started without warning one day as he approached his one-year anniversary of arriving on the island. All morning he could hear P. I.'s voice barking out orders to the servants. There was a constant hum of activity coming from the factory, though he had no idea what was behind it all. For once he was grateful to be out in the heat, struggling with his shovel to excavate another hole for a lime tree. As long as P. I. was shouting in the factory, he felt safe.

In the afternoon, after a particularly loud and long volley of shouting from P. I., John's supervisor looked startled and hurried back in the direction of the factory. At first John carried on digging, though a little slower than usual. But when what felt like an hour had passed and John remained alone, he decided that it was safe enough to leave.

He walked, as quietly as his leg chain would allow, back to his shack and carefully retrieved his copy of Euclid. He could hear voices nearby and paused in the doorway, scanning the area in case anyone might see him. When he was sure it was safe to leave, he hurried away to one of the far beaches.

He found a stick, sat down on the sand, and opened the book to one of his favorite pages, a series of diagrams and text that explained Euclid's theory for establishing the circumference of a circle. John found it comforting to copy out the page right there on the sand. The world of mathematics was clear and simple. It was a world that always followed the rules. It was predictable and honest. It was safe.

John held his legs tight to his chest, closed his eyes, and let himself rock gently from side to side. The motion reminded him of the rocking of the waves, but it sparked another memory as well. A memory of being a small child, unable to sleep for the terrors that stalked his dreams. His mother would lay beside him, rocking gently back and forth as she reminded him to pray.

"You!"

The shout startled him instantly. He opened his eyes expecting to see Evans, but instead it was a man that John had never seen before. He was European, and English, too, by the sound of him. He was standing close enough for John to see that he was a little older than Evans, by the looks of him, with his hand shielded against the sun as he stared in John's direction.

After almost a year of being in Evans's possession—most of the time in leg chains—John had lost the instinct to run. Instead, he sat motionless, hoping that the man, whoever he was, would lose interest and walk away.

He didn't. Instead, he started to walk in John's direction.

"Hello?" The man was calling to him, but John could not answer.

The closer he got, the more fearful John became. The anxiety clawed at his throat, making it hard to breathe.

"Are you English? Can you hear me?"

He was close enough for John to see clearly now. His sailor's hands, his weather-beaten face. John tried to get to his feet, but his chain got caught up on itself and he stumbled back onto the sand.

John kept his eyes closed, willing the man to disappear. He could sense him approaching even closer, hear his feet upon the sand. When the man stopped walking, he was so close that John could smell the tobacco and sweat that hovered about him. He could feel the sunlight disappear as he slipped beneath the man's shadow.

John could tell that the man was crouching beside him now. He was so close that John could feel him just inches away. John wanted nothing more than to disappear, but something was compelling him to look. He opened his eyes and stared into the face that was looking back at him.

It had been so long since anyone had stared at John with kindness or pity that he had forgotten what it looked like.

John gazed back, trying to read the stranger's face.

"What *are* you?"

It was not pity on the man's face. It was not kindness either. It was revulsion.

Inside, John could feel himself breaking apart.

For Mr. Patrick Clow—undoubtedly one of the premier traders in the Kittam region of the Guinea coast—his first visit to Plantain Island was full of surprises.

First, there was Evans. Patrick had encountered him once before, perhaps twice. Either way, Patrick had never thought much of him as a trader. It was common knowledge that he paddled his bedraggled shallop up and down the Sherbro River, the heart of the Bullom people's territory. Every trader within a hundred miles knew that the Bullom people were devils to trade with, and any man who attempted it was clearly a fool. He was a small man with strange ideas, and Patrick shared the commonly held belief that Evans would be out of business within a year. Perhaps two.

And yet, as Evans's factory on Plantain Island had opened for business, word soon spread. Evans had built a large factory on one corner of Plantain Island and was looking for other traders to build their own factories there too. People used words like *ambition* and *impressive*, though others declared it *folly*. Either way, Patrick was intrigued and sent word to the island announcing his intention to visit.

When he first set foot on the island and saw the extent of the factory Evans had built, he was convinced that the gossip was right. Evans was clearly a fool, and an arrogant one at that. No man in his right mind would believe that he could fill so large a factory by trading solely with the Bullom. The handful of slaves that he could purchase on each trip would rattle around with too much space and would surely get up to mischief. Traders would arrive, see the scale of the factory, and assume they would be able to come away with a dozen or more blacks at a time. Evans would be lucky if he could sell them two. Any man who accepted Evans's invitation to set up business on the Plantains would be doomed to share the same disastrous fate.

And then, having offered a seat in the shade and a glass of rum, Evans introduced her. A woman of such poise and charm and cold-eyed determination that Patrick was instantly impressed. But it was when he heard her name—Princess P. I. of the Bombo family—and heard it announced that she was his wife, that he had been forced right there and then to reassess everything he had ever thought about Evans. Going into partnership with the daughter of the chief of the Bullom people was a trading masterstroke. It would instantly guarantee a steady supply of stock.

That was not all. The princess was magnificent. The more he listened to her—her eyes never breaking with his—the more he understood that finally, he had a true competitor in business to contend with.

Of course, he had held her gaze and given nothing away. He conversed more in the European style than the African, trading insipid pleasantries as he probed for any sign of weakness that he could use to his advantage. He could find none.

Patrick could feel the sweat on his back. He was grateful when Evans stood up and suggested a closer inspection of what was currently for sale.

"Yes," added the princess. "You are welcome here. We are not adversaries. There is more than enough room on the island for other factories. Together we can prosper."

"My good lady," Patrick purred, "I could not agree with you more. To share this island with you in business would be an honor. I would welcome the opportunity to view your stock."

They were magnificent. Twenty of them, and not a single one sick or weak or defective in any way. They were so healthy and looked so strong that Patrick was convinced that almost all of them would make it across the Middle Passage alive.

"Well," he said as Princess P. I. and Evans invited him to share a second glass of rum once the inspection was over, "I must congratulate you. But no, I cannot stay. I have urgent business to attend to back at one of my own factories in Kittam. Another time, perhaps."

There was no urgent business to attend to, but he did want to leave. He wanted to leave and never come back. More importantly, he wanted to make sure that none of the other traders in the area took up Evans's offer either. It would take some planning, but it was essential that he succeed. Evans must not be allowed to grow his business.

But then, as he walked the long way round the island back to his shallop— all the time imagining how vast the business could grow on the Plantains and wondering how he could stop it—he saw the most surprising thing of all.

A white man, shackled like a common prisoner.

At first he thought his eyes were deceiving him. But as he called out to the man—though the poor fellow was barely worthy of such a term—Patrick saw that he was right. The man was young, perhaps no older than twenty-five, but his skin bore the marks of one who had spent years exposed to the elements. He was wild, dressed in rags, rocking himself back and forth.

Patrick approached, more out of curiosity than compassion. The man tried to move but tripped and fell.

Patrick crouched beside him, and the man finally opened his eyes. They were wild and frantic, full of fear.

"What *are* you?" Patrick asked. It was a simple question, but it struck the man like an arrow. He clamped his eyes shut and threw himself back onto the sand, whispering over and over to himself.

And that was when Patrick encountered the biggest surprise of all. The man was English.

"A servant of slaves," the man said. "A servant of slaves. She has broken me all into pieces."

The smell was foul, and Patrick wanted to leave, but as he looked at the sand, he decided to stay right where he was. There were strange drawings etched out all around the man, and a copy of an English book of mathematical problems.

Patrick sat back and let himself think. Apart from Evans, P. I., and their people, there was nobody else living on the island. It was too small for anyone to be living on it without their knowledge, so this wretch of a man must have had something to do with them.

"Who is this 'she' you mention?" he asked. "You mean Princess P. I.?"

The whispering stopped, replaced by a long, low groan. A sound of fear and pain that was barely human.

Patrick waited. He waited for the groaning to ease. For the sun to arc farther across the sky. For his mind to settle on a plan of action that would allow him to use this man to his advantage.

It took time for John to decide to trust Patrick Clow, yet the businessman was as perceptive as he was persuasive. He returned to meet with Evans and P. I. on the island several times after his first visit, and on each occasion he was sure to seek John out and spend a little time with him. He showed John great kindness, bringing him food and new clothes at first. He talked to him about news from back in England—of the war with the French and the escape of Bonnie Prince Charlie—and reminded John what it felt like to be treated as an equal. He persuaded Evans to do away with the ankle chains. Piece by piece, John could feel himself growing back together again.

Finally, months after Patrick's first visit, he explained his plan to John. He had persuaded P. I. and Evans to part with him (not that they had taken much persuading), and his desire was that John would agree to manage the new factory that he was building on the island.

At first, John was unsure. Patrick's offer was tempting, that much he knew for sure. John craved the opportunity to be freed from the abuses of P. I. and Evans. But managing a factory of his own? There were times when he could barely remember his own name, let alone take charge of others. To do so on Plantain Island, under the noses of the very couple who had made it their mission to reduce him to so wretched a state, it felt like a task he could never accomplish.

"Should you make a success of the factory here"—he added, careful that nobody could overhear them—"I shall be more than happy to move you to one of my larger factories on the shore. Work hard for me, John, and I promise that eventually you will never have to see either of them again."

It was all John needed to hear. He agreed and began work immediately.

As a factory manager his tasks were simple enough. All he had to do was make sure that the slaves Patrick delivered from time to time were held securely. He fed them daily, made sure that they were ready for sale as requested. It was easy work, far easier than struggling to break rock and plant lime trees.

Patrick was as good as his word. As soon as he returned to the island and saw that John was not the broken wretch he had first encountered on the beach but a reliable, hardworking man—who was also more than happy to reveal everything he knew about Evans, P. I., and their business together—he transferred John to his factory on the Kittam River.

The journey of more than a hundred miles south from Plantain Island took a little more than a few days, but it could have been years. Knowing that he was free from Evans and P. I. was deeply comforting, and just sailing itself was a tonic to his wounded soul. South of Sherbro Island, he left the estuary to follow the winding Kittam River as it snaked along parallel to the coast for thirty or forty miles. By the time John stepped off the boat and onto the shore, he felt like an entirely different man. He was in Kittam now, the lowland region far upstream that took its name from the river, where it bent back closest to the Atlantic. The last of the fear and anxiety had gone, and most of his old confidence had returned.

The sense of this being a new beginning was increased by the vast differences between Patrick's factory at Kittam and the operations back on Plantain Island. Previously, John's experience of running a factory had led him to believe that it was a simple task. All that it required was the ability to unlock and lock a door.

From the start, it was clear that he had a lot to learn, especially when it came to business. The Kittam factory was so much bigger than Evans's, and much better fortified. Instead of being constructed out of palm trees, the walls were made of stone.

"To stop them getting out," said Patrick when he noticed John staring. "And to stop others getting in."

The biggest difference was what went on outside the factory walls. Back on the island, both Evans's and Patrick Clow's purchase of stock took place far away, either up the Rio Nuña or the Sherbro or elsewhere. John had never dealt with local traders before. At Kittam they were regular visitors, and negotiating with them was both complicated and volatile. He had barely been there a week when he saw his first trade between his master and a black trader. The local was offering a pair of young females, and after examining them his boss had questioned whether they really were quite as healthy as the trader said they were.

"What do you think I am?" the local trader screamed, jumping up and overturning the table in front of him. "A white man?"

The deal was done eventually, and it led to a lengthy discussion with Patrick about the way he conducted his trade.

"These local traders will cheat and lie and do everything they can to deceive us. And we are the same with them. We dilute the rum with water, put false heads in the gunpowder kegs, and remove as much as half the cotton from the bales. Everything about this trade is based on a lie. They know it and we know it. There can be no other way."

The factory itself was like a busy village on the Kittam River. It was a hub for all kinds of traders, not just those who dealt in slaves, and there was a constantly changing cast of characters around him. Previously, apart from Evans he had been surrounded exclusively by people from the Bullom tribe. The Kittam region was a melting pot by comparison, with Muslim Mandingos from the inland north, and Mande-speaking Vai and Mende tribes from the inland south—all competing and gathering to trade, along with smaller tribes, and all placing pressure on the local Sherbro people, as the south Bulloms were called. There were also the regular visits from European Guinea traders who would anchor off the coast and row ashore for business. Though on a river, connected to a vast system of inland waterways, the factory was still only a mile from the coast. It was the best of both worlds for a trader.

John no longer hid in shame when he saw white people. He had a job to do. Thanks to Patrick he had status. When traders and locals looked at him, there was no pity or revulsion. From some, there was respect. From others, a little fear.

John adjusted to his new life quickly, yet he was surprised when after a week Patrick announced that he was heading north on business. He left John in charge of the factory, both the dozen slaves and the storeroom full of rum, gunpowder, and cotton for trade—goods that John calculated were worth thousands of pounds. In less than three months he had gone from servant of slaves to manager of a small fortune. The change was dizzying. He wanted more.

There was a phrase that John had heard Captain Phelps use from time to time when he was on board the *Levant*, a term that had always confused him. The captain used it to describe the way that European traders who spent years on the Guinea coast were changed by their experiences, saying of these white men that they had "grown black." Since John had never actually seen any of the people Captain Phelps described, he was unable to say whether the term referred to a change in skin color or some other type of transformation, and he chose not to dwell on it. Yet for some unknown reason, as he settled into his new life in Kittam, the phrase returned to his thoughts. Whatever "growing black" meant, he suspected that Kittam was precisely the kind of place where it could happen.

John was never sure of the precise moment when that same change started for him, but before long he knew without a doubt that his own transition was underway. He knew it on the day he first traded with a local, lying successfully about the quality of the rum he was selling—rum that only hours before he had been carefully mixing with a blend of boiled water and palm wine. He knew it, too, when the same traders invited him to drink with them later that night, sharing their own, highly fortified palm wine with him.

He could feel the change strengthening when he walked about the village and nobody stared at him. It was there the day he realized he was happier squatting on his heels while he worked rather than sitting in the dirt like a dog. He knew it when the mosquito bites no longer itched quite so much.

After living so long like a slave—from the time he was press-ganged onto the *Harwich* to the dark days on the Plantains—John had almost forgotten what pleasure felt like. Kittam offered him all manner of comforts. All of his appetites could be satisfied—all of them.

Then there was the time Patrick took him inland on a special voyage to trade. There was no fear in John as the sound of the ocean receded. No fear as they slipped farther and farther inland. Africa no longer terrified him, though he knew there was much terror within her.

He and Patrick traveled from village to village, doing business with local chiefs in the day and sleeping in their compounds at night. Though his grasp of the various languages and dialects was poor, John understood well enough that he and Patrick were perfectly safe whenever they were welcomed in by an elder.

There was a day that stood out above all others, a day when John found himself deep inland, far from the river. They were in the largest settlement he had ever seen, a town with tall wooden structures as high as a London house. There were drummers at the top, pounding their wild, incessant rhythms as strong as an Atlantic winter swell. He marveled at it all, wide-eyed and amazed just like he had been as a child down by the docks. It was a new world he had discovered, and just like before, he felt its lure on him.

There was some kind of religious ceremony taking place, but it was unlike any church service he had ever encountered at home. It started before dawn, with the drummers calling people to gather. They sat in small groups, some under trees, some out in the open. When the drumming stopped, all of them lifted up their hands as if they were holding something precious before them.

They stayed like that for hours. Nobody spoke, nobody moved.

When it was over and Patrick announced that it was time for them to leave, John wondered out loud whether he might return again someday.

Patrick stopped and looked at him.

"Men like you and me," he said, a half-smile resting on his face, "we always return. We will never leave."

Chapter 6 ——————— Storm (1747–1748)

John was unhappy about being woken so early in the day, but his younger co-worker was insistent.

"A ship. I seen a ship passing by and made the signal that we wished to trade. But now it is closer I see it is no slaver," he repeated from outside John's door. "Please, Mr. Newton. I do not know what to do."

John dressed clumsily, though he was careful not to disturb the bed's other occupant. He hurried up to the lookout point near the factory, blinking in the bright sunshine as he adjusted the spyglass.

John studied the ship carefully. It was a merchant vessel but had none of the usual features of a Guinea ship. There was no *barricado* to protect the crew, no nets around the edge to protect the profits. It was just as his co-worker had said.

It wasn't unheard of for a non-slave trading merchant to venture down toward Kittam, but it was unusual. Months had passed since he last encountered one.

"They may not be buying," John said to him, "but if they are selling rum and cotton, we might be interested. Row out to them if they drop anchor, see what they have." He waited until he could see the ship signal its intent to stop, then went back to bed.

He was in an even deeper sleep an hour later when there was a knock on his door again. This time it was even more insistent. Within minutes John stood outside his factory, shocked and dumbfounded as he asked Captain Anthony Gother of the *Greyhound* to repeat himself.

"Your father wrote to his friend Joseph Manesty, of Liverpool, owner of the *Greyhound* and my employer. Your father informed him that you were somewhere on the Guinea coast and urged him to do what he could to help you. Mr. Manesty sent us with instructions to search for you as we traded. We left Liverpool nearly seven months ago now, started trading at Gambia, and then worked our way down the coast. And now, all of a sudden, here you are! I cannot believe that we have found you."

"No," said John, still confused by events. "No. It is . . . remarkable. How did you find me again?"

"Every trading post where we have stopped, I have asked if any man there has heard of John Newton. We called at Sierra Leone and the Banana Islands, but there was no word of you. I quite gave you up for dead or lost. But here you are, alive and very much found! I daresay Mr. Manesty will be almost as delighted as your father. Now, how soon can you be ready to depart?"

"Depart?"

"Yes. We are buying beeswax and camwood and the like, not slaves, but we have not yet finished trading. I want to travel farther south as far as Gabon at the Equator before crossing to Brazil. With good winds we should have you back in England within a year."

"No," said John, his voice instantly rid of the confusion and hesitation. His life in England was so distant that it had faded almost completely from his memory. To return to it was as impossible as returning to his own childhood. "No, Captain. I will not be sailing with you."

"But Mr. Manesty's instructions were quite clear. If we find you, I must bring you home."

"I am grateful to you for searching so diligently, Captain Gother. But I cannot leave." John's eyes flicked back to the doorway and the bedroom beyond it. "I live here now. This is where I shall remain."

The captain closed his eyes, took a deep breath, and shook his head, like he was trying to erase a thought from his mind. "Mr. Newton, I must ask your forgiveness. I neglected to tell you that there is one further reason why your father was so keen for you to return. I must apologize, but in our haste, we left Liverpool without a series of letters, one of which is from your father, informing you that you have been named beneficiary in a relative's will."

"Who?"

"I . . . I . . ." Captain Gother stammered, "I do not recall fully, though I believe it was a distant relative and their passing was not unexpected. However, I do know that it is a substantial amount."

"Substantial?"

"Yes," the captain smiled, leaning a little closer as he dropped his voice. "Some £400 per annum, I believe. A fortune like that is more than enough for you to build a new life for yourself in England."

He continued talking, but John's thoughts drifted.

Almost two years had passed since John had last seen either Polly or his father. At first, when he was on board the *Harwich* as it patrolled the waters of the English Channel, it was easy to hold on to the hope of returning to his old life once more. It was all a matter of will, of determination. As long as he could find a way to fight himself free from the navy, he was sure that eventually he would rebuild his career and win Polly's hand in marriage. But the farther south he had sailed, the farther away from England he drifted, the fainter his old ambitions became. Between the flogging on the *Harwich*, the humiliation he had endured at the hands of P. I. and Evans, and the five months spent giving himself over to life in Kittam, John was sure that there was almost no trace of his old self left within him. None of his plans. None of his self-belief. None of his ideals.

And yet, as the captain of the *Greyhound* continued offering descriptions of the type of life a newly wealthy man could look forward to back in England, John could feel the old hopes and ambitions awaken. They were faint and they were feeble, but they were alive.

"You will be a rich man with such an inheritance," Captain Gother continued. "Certainly rich enough to compensate for any . . . pleasures that you have to leave behind here."

John could feel himself softening.

"And at the request of Mr. Manesty, you shall lodge in my cabin and eat at my table. You shall be my constant companion for the duration of the voyage and never once will I expect any service from you. Aboard the *Greyhound* you shall be a man of leisure, Mr. Newton. Consider it good training for the new life that awaits you when you finally set foot on English soil once more."

John smiled.

"Hah!" said the captain, clapping his hand on John's shoulder. "I knew you would see sense. This is a marvelous opportunity for you, Mr. Newton. A marvelous opportunity indeed."

Eleven months later, on the day that he finally decided the *Greyhound* was ready to head west across the Atlantic, Captain Gother stood on deck outside his cabin and battled the urge to despair. It was a scene that had become depressingly familiar of late. A scene which could only spell trouble.

After more than a year trading north and south along the west African coast—at one point traveling more than a thousand miles south of Kittam—the *Greyhound* was full. The hold was packed tight with camwood, beeswax, gold, and ivory, and there was not a single square foot of space left to be filled. This was not a slave ship, but they had nevertheless survived countless dangers, from the hidden reefs that littered the coast to the crooked traders who would happily steal and murder if they thought they could increase their profits. The voyage so far had been a success way beyond his expectations, and yet despair threatened to suffocate him completely.

Gother knew precisely why the journey was troubling him so. He knew precisely when and where things went wrong as well.

Kittam.

The day he charmed and cajoled and lied in the hope of persuading Newton aboard.

At first, his cabin guest had been no trouble. Newton had spent most of his days either reading or standing on deck, watching the coast drift by. But the longer their voyage continued, the more restless Newton had become. He retreated into the books that Gother offered him to read but found little joy or distraction in them. Newton brooded over the pages and became more and more withdrawn from the rest of the crew.

The only thing that appeared to ease Newton's mood was being on deck, especially in the evening when they were at anchor. With the crew assembled and the rum flowing freely, Newton would join in with the singing and laughter. All he needed was good company, thought Gother. And who could blame him? Gother had seen plenty of men grown black. To return to England after giving yourself to life in Africa was no mean feat. Newton would need a little support.

As the trading continued and the long months crept by, the captain noticed a change. Newton was no longer content simply to nurse a drink and smile at the bawdy songs that filled the night sky. Newton's voice became one of the loudest ones on deck. He might not be the first to call for more rum, but his laugh was more raucous and lasted longer than any of the others.

Then there were the songs. Several months after they collected him at Kittam, Newton started improvising drinking songs. The captain heard a few of them and found them funny enough, if a little vulgar. He also suspected that there were other songs in Newton's repertoire—worse ones, no doubt—that were only sung when he was out of earshot.

There was at least one incident when the drinking got out of hand as well. Though the captain never witnessed it directly, he heard the rumors about a night when Newton was so drunk he leapt off the ship, only to be pulled back at the last minute by a crew member marginally less drunk.

If there was one thing that troubled the captain more than the fluctuating moods or nighttime drinking, it was Newton's influence on the crew. He could barely utter a single sentence without resorting to profanities, and he had a particular disdain for anyone who declared himself a serious Christian. The way he bitterly denounced the most sacred things, mocked the Bible as primitive and untrue, and poured scorn on all that was most holy—it sent a shudder through his body.

And so, on the day that he decided that they had done business enough in Africa and that Brazil now beckoned, with the trade winds that would carry them there and all the way home, Captain Gother had been feeling good. He had enjoyed standing on the deck, announcing to the crew that the first stage of their long journey was now over. He had relished the opportunity to tell them that they had all served well and would enjoy a new barrel of rum to help them celebrate that night. But then, almost in an instant, the mood had soured.

Newton decided to make up a new lyric right there and then. It ridiculed one of his oldest and most reliable of men. Everyone laughed—except the old man and Captain Gother.

"That man," said the exasperated captain to no one in particular. "That man is a Jonah. To sail with him is to sail under a permanent curse."

John was well aware of the consequences of the *Greyhound* spending so long trading along the African coast. It was plain for all to see, even for a dullard like Captain Gother. A year marinating in the heat and humidity of the equatorial waters had caused significant damage to almost every part of the ship. The sails were growing thin, the rigging was starting to degrade, and many of the timbers down at water level were showing early signs of rot. Even the sheep, pig, and chicken pens that covered the deck had grown fragile and there were regular escapes from their livestock.

After so long at sea the *Greyhound* needed a comprehensive overhaul. It needed to be taken to a dock and have the decks and spars scraped, caulked, tarred, or painted, the rigging overhauled, and the sails replaced or mended. And yet instead of pausing a few more weeks, delayed in a port on the coast and making the necessary repairs, the captain had decided to embark on a seven-thousand-mile journey arcing across the Atlantic. They would take on water and provisions at the small volcanic island of Annobón in the Gulf of Guinea, some two hundred miles west of Cape Lopez on the coast. They would sail to within sight of Brazil and up through the West Indies, then onto the Newfoundland Banks before cresting back eastward across the Atlantic a second time in a handful of weeks. Because they had no slave cargo to deliver, they could return to England in one long voyage. It was as foolish a decision as any John had ever witnessed.

John tried to recommend an alternative route, but the captain was deaf to advice, no matter how many times he offered it. Eventually, when the middle passage was complete, John decided there was no use talking to the man, and so he dedicated himself to making the crew happy instead. He made them laugh at every opportunity. It was good to feel like he had a purpose.

And yet John knew what was really going on. It wasn't simply the perilous state of the ship that was troubling him. It was the state of his soul. He was as worn out, as threadbare, and as weak and fragile as the *Greyhound* itself. He was returning home to the father on whom he had brought great shame and the young woman whose love he had betrayed. The chains that had once been clamped around his ankles were long since gone, yet he had never felt more like a wretch.

All the way north from Brazil he could feel the weight in his chest. At times it made it hard to eat, to sleep, even to breathe. It was always there. Nothing could ease it. This looming fear and unease that had taken up residence within him was not within his control.

In time even the old distractions that used to work—the songs and the laughter and the drinking with the rest of his friends on the crew—started to taste stale to him. They became like the old, maggot-infested hard tack that he was given in the bowels of the *Harwich*. Nothing was good anymore. Nothing helped. Everything felt wrong.

John retreated to whatever corner of the ship where he could be alone. He tried writing again, drafting over and over a letter to Polly to be sent when they finally landed in Liverpool. If he could find the right words to send to her first, then perhaps he might be able to prepare her for his arrival. But how to begin? How to explain everything that had happened these last three years?

The words refused to come.

There was nothing to say.

It was late February, almost two months since they had left Africa. Captain Gother declared that the *Greyhound* would pause its journey for a half day on the Grand Banks off Newfoundland. He said that with clear skies above and the temperature just a fraction below freezing and a gentle north easterly breeze to contend with, the conditions were almost perfect for a spot of cod fishing.

Having spent so long in Africa, John suffered more than most in the arctic wind. The time that he had spent chained up on the deck of Evans's shallop had left its mark. After so many nights when he shivered from dusk until dawn in the wind and the rain, he had developed a vulnerability to the cold. It stalked him, tormented him, attacking his very bones as soon as the temperature dipped.

At first John tried to join in with the fishing, but his hands were soon too numb to grasp the handline. He tried to help the men who were preparing the cod—gutting them and packing them in barrels of salt—but his lifeless fingers fumbled with the knife. He remained on deck for as long as he could, but the pain that raced through his bones soon drove him to take shelter.

It was a little less cold in the cabin, but thawing out didn't make John feel much better. The stabbing pains had gone, and he was no longer shivering quite so uncontrollably, but the dark thoughts and feelings returned.

He tried to distract himself with thoughts about the coming months. Home was close now, only a matter of three or four weeks sailing with a good wind. Soon they would be arriving in Liverpool and within days John would be returning to Aveley to see his father. He would learn the identity of his mysterious benefactor, and before long he would be able to embark on his new life as a man with £400 to try to spend every year. There was everything to look forward to, but still he was troubled.

In search of distraction, John tried reading. He had already worked his way through most of the books in the captain's library. None had been able to offer him the kind of escape he craved. He selected one of the few he had not yet touched, *The Imitation of Jesus Christ* by Thomas à Kempis. The book itself was old and dog-eared, a much-loved copy that had inspired countless readers. John tried to study it. He wanted to open himself to the deep truths within its pages, to be one of those readers on whom it left its mark, but it was no use. The shivering returned, just like when he was on deck. He could not hold the pages steady enough to see the words.

Leaving the Newfoundland waters at the beginning of March, they headed east into the cold North Atlantic, making for home. The temperatures lifted marginally, and a strong wind pushed them on into darker skies ahead. With every day that passed, the pressure inside John increased. He rarely left the cabin, and when Captain Gother was present the two men only ever exchanged a few words at a time. Once John thought he heard the captain call him Jonah.

At the start of the second week in March, John was struggling. They were about ten days' sail to reach England by his reckoning, but with each passing day he felt more troubled. He was tired, yet sleep refused to come. He was cold but could not get warm. His heart raced, but nothing he did could make it slow. Peace was as distant a memory as his childhood wanderings along the Thames.

Feeling desperate, he returned to Thomas à Kempis. For once he could concentrate long enough to read a few pages, and he found that he could begin to digest the words. He read on, hungry for some truth or comfort that would help.

The book only made him feel worse.

Life is brief, he read. Our grip on it is weak. We might think that we are strong, but we are all sinners. And one day every one of us will be called upon to account for our actions.

"Ah, wretched guilty creature," he read, feeling the words take root deep within him. "Ah, stupid unthinking sinner! How shalt thou escape the terrors of that dreadful day?"

A moment of clarity settled on him.

If this is true, he reasoned, then what man could be a greater sinner than me? I have turned my back on God. I have embraced everything that I once thought was wrong. I have no hope of salvation.

All day the thoughts plagued him. By the time darkness settled, despair had overwhelmed him completely. He was returning home, yet he had never felt more lost.

He tried to sleep, but his body would not obey.

By candlelight he tried writing, but the pen felt as lifeless and awkward as the knife in his frozen fingers.

Desperate, he picked up Thomas à Kempis again, hoping to find something new within the pages that might offer some kind of help. There was nothing in the book for him. Only the same words that he'd read earlier. Sin creates a debt. Soon or later, the debt must be paid.

He slammed the book down on the table.

"I have made my choice," he said.

John woke to a cold blast of wind and seawater.

"Storm!" yelled one of the crew as he descended the ladder into the cabin and searched frantically among the captain's possessions by the light of a wildly swaying lamp. "The ship is sinking! Get out there and help!"

John leapt out of bed and started to climb the ladder, struggling to keep his balance as the ship lurched from side to side. It was three in the morning.

"Go back!" A voice shouted at him from above.

He looked up and saw the captain's form filling the hatch above him. His face was wild and desperate. Between him and the dark sky above John could see the tattered remnants of the sail whipping in air. "I need a knife, Newton. Fetch me one from my chest."

John turned back and joined in the search, holding the lamp while the sailor who had roused him emptied the chest.

"I have it!" his crewmate shouted before barreling up the ladder.

John was right behind him, hands clamped tight on each rung. He was about to take the final step off the ladder and onto the main deck when a mighty wave rolled over the ship, sweeping the first sailor from his feet. His screams, as well as the cries of most of the livestock as they were hurled from the ship, vanished as soon as he was swallowed by the raging sea.

Somewhere nearby John heard timber breaking apart. There was more shouting and screaming.

John stood frozen, hoping he was dreaming, but knowing it was real.

"Newton!" the captain yelled, pointing to the hold. "Help with the pumps!"

Another wave swept the last of the pigs and sheep overboard. John hurried as best he could over to the one man—lashed to the gunnel—operating one of the two pumps that were fixed to the deck near the entrance to the hold. John looked into the hold and saw that it was full of water.

"Tie yourself on," shouted the sailor, nodding to a length of rope nearby. "We can't afford to lose any more men."

For the next hour John operated the second pump. The sea continued to pitch the *Greyhound* violently in all directions. Waves routinely surged over them, and more than once John lost his footing and was only saved by the rope. The wind whipped seawater and rain into his eyes, and the sound of breaking timber caused the rest of the men to shout and scream in terror.

Only when there were flashes of lightning could John see clearly. The waves above them, as tall as a cathedral. The sails in shreds, clinging weakly to the masts. The rest of the crew—those lucky enough to have survived—all exhausted, some frantic and hysterical as they fought for survival.

It was three in the morning when John started pumping, and he continued through dawn and into the morning. The storm eased a little around daylight, but the relief they felt was only temporary. Finally, they could see the full extent of the damage. A large section of the upper bow of the ship was smashed and letting in water. The sails were almost completely ruined. Nothing that had not been tied to the deck remained—none of the livestock, none of the supplies. One of the crew had already been swept to his death.

The worst of the storm might have been over, but the fear was just as strong as it had been when the waves were breaking over their heads. The *Greyhound* was still crashing downward as the waves gave way, from peak to valley, and each time the hull creaked and groaned and threatened to break up entirely.

Some of the crew were working frantically to bail and pump the water out from the hold. Others were desperately wadding holes with any spare clothes they could find, nailing boards of wood over top as a crude patch. All on board appeared to have lost any hope of survival.

Having struggled under the weight of despair for so many weeks, John wanted to offer some comfort to the crew.

"Think about it, men," he called out. "In a few days we will be safe and warm at port. We will have wine in our bellies and laughter on our faces as we recount the tale of how we survived the greatest storm any of us have ever faced. They will be lining up outside the taverns to hear us, mark my words."

"No," said one sailor nearby. "In a few hours we shall be buried beneath the waves. The ship is weakened beyond all measure. We are exhausted. The instant the gale picks up again the sea will claim us. There is no hope for us."

Nobody spoke after that. It troubled John to see the men so fearful, but he knew they were right. The *Greyhound* was lost. If it hadn't been for all the camwood and beeswax crammed in the hold, it would have sunk already.

He glanced at the damage on the starboard side of the bow where the ship had been shattered. There was a gaping hole where the upper timbers should have been. John thought about the danger of being swamped again. With some urgency, he untied himself from the gunnel and went to talk to the captain at the helm.

"We must change our heading," John shouted over the noise of the wind. "No matter how off course it takes us, we must keep the ruined section of the bow high out of the water."

Captain Gother wiped the sweat from his eyes. "We could try. What else can we do?"

John nodded. "If it will not help us stay afloat, the Lord have mercy on us."

The instant the words left his mouth, John was stunned. He stumbled back to his position at the pump, shocked that he had just called on God for mercy. Did that mean that somewhere inside, a part of him still believed that God might choose to save them? And if he did still have eternal hope, was he nothing more than a poor, deluded fool?

He lashed himself back to the gunnel and resumed pumping, questions flashing like lightning across his mind. He thought about mercy and justice, punishment and sin. He wondered what would happen if the ship sank and he drowned. Would he be sent to hell for all he had done?

He wondered what would happen if he survived. Would it mean that God had chosen to save him? And if that was true, why?

All day John worked at the pump. His hands were bleeding, his body shivering in the cold.

In the afternoon the captain sent John back to the cabin to sleep for an hour. He lay down on the mattress that was cold and wet with seawater and closed his eyes. He had no idea whether he would wake up again, and a part of him did not care either way. There were no answers to his questions, not yet at least. Life was in the balance. Death could come at any moment. Then he would know.

At three he was shaken awake and told to take over from the captain at the helm. The waves were picking up again and he steered until midnight, not so much to follow a course of any kind, but simply to keep the damaged section of the hull away from the worst of the waves.

This time, his mind was full of memories from his childhood. Times when he sat beside his mother while at church. The memory of the softness of her cotton dress. The way her voice soared when she sang. The way she placed every ounce of her attention on the preacher as he stood up to speak.

Some of those sermons came back to him as well. He could hear his childhood pastor, David Jennings, and picture the chapel at Wapping. He remembered being warned against sin and temptation so many times. There were calls to surrender at the foot of the cross as well. The guidance had been there, constant and consistent, yet since leaving England he knew that he had lived as though he had never stepped foot in a church. Not even once. He might as well have been an infidel.

All day and all evening he manned the helm, and as he piloted the battered ship, he tried to find a way to keep what little faith he had mustered afloat too.

It was not easy. Especially when he noticed that the rest of the crew had slipped further into their own despair.

"There is nothing else to decide," one man concluded after emerging from the hold and informing the crew that all provisions were now perished. "Either we starve to death, or we will be forced before long to eat each other."

Murmurs of agreement went around the crew. John expected Captain Gother to step in and say something to reassure the men. The captain remained silent, walking slowly around the ship, staring at the damage.

"Captain," John said quietly as he passed nearby. "Our sufferings are light compared to our fears. These men need reassurance and comfort from you."

The captain stopped and stared John in the eye. "You are the sole cause of the calamity. You alone. You are the Jonah that has brought this horror upon us."

Four days after the storm, conditions on the *Greyhound* remained dire. While they had several barrels of drinking water in the hold and a few on deck and a little brandy, there was no food apart from a little bread, the salted cod they had caught off the Banks of Newfoundland, and a small quantity of pig feed. What was left of the sails was so ragged and torn that any strips of canvas left were best used to try to plug the holes in the hull that were continually letting in sea water. This left the ship lifeless, without any means of propulsion, virtually dead in the water. All they could do was hope that the gentle westerly wind at their backs would continue, while not mounting into anything more dangerous.

The crew were largely silent as they went about their work of bailing, pumping, and replugging the holes that were constantly opening up like seeping wounds. Captain Gother let slip the odd comment to the crew about John being like Jonah, but most of the time he was quiet and solemn. Like the captain, the whole ship was subdued. The crew was like a condemned man waiting to be sent to the gallows.

John was just as silent as the rest, but his mind was far away from this scene of threatened death and despair. The gloom he felt had lifted.

Instead, he was contemplating the remarkable gift of life.

It had taken a few days, but as it became clear that the ship might not sink after all, it slowly dawned on him that there was only one possible explanation for their survival. God had saved them.

When he wasn't working alongside the crew, John retreated to the cabin, reading a New Testament and a book of sermons from the captain's library. Some of the words he read struck him with such force that he had to pause and close his eyes for a moment.

We can read over the whole history of the Savior's passion with dry eyes, and be no more troubled at it as if we had been no way concerned in it.

That was him. He had done that, even in that very cabin, less than one month before. He had lived that way for years too, fully aware yet utterly indifferent to the death of Jesus.

Shall we still live in sin, notwithstanding that our Lord has died for it . . . ?

It is He who supports our spirits and carries us with patience and comfort through it. When we are in straits, and know not which way to take, it is He who guides us by His counsel and directs us by His Holy Spirit, to what is most for His glory and our good . . .

Reading such words was like discovering a map that revealed not only exactly where he had been, but where he wanted to go.

When we are heavy laden with the burden of our sins, it is He who gives rest and quiet to our souls.

Early on the fifth day after the storm, just as the sun was rising ahead of them, the man on lookout let out an almighty shout. "Land ahoy! Land ahoy! I see it there in the distance. Look!"

The pumping and bailing and repairing paused as every man strained for a better look.

"Mountains," said one.

"The Blue Stacks," said another. "North of Donegal Bay. I'd know them anywhere."

"Two days at most with this wind behind us, lads," said the captain. "And we'll be there. Let's have a drink!"

The last of the brandy was shared out, a pint for every man. They drank and stared and smiled and cheered at the thought of cheating death.

Slowly, as the sun continued its gentle rise into the sky, the cheering and the smiling lessened. Then faded into nothing. Within thirty minutes it was clear. There were no mountains in the distance. They were only clouds.

"Fear not, lads," said the captain. "Land cannot be far away."

His words fell on deaf ears and stone hearts. As quickly as joy had arrived that morning, despair now settled upon the crew.

The next day, the gentle wind that had been with them since the storm ended was gone. The air was still and lifeless. They were becalmed. Without the westerly pushing at their ragged hull, they were left drifting, motionless and trapped in the middle of the ocean. Dead in the water.

With both the brandy and bread now gone, the captain cut the rations further. A handful of cod, a little less of pig grain—this was all each man was allowed. Nobody complained. Nobody had the energy.

On the sixth day following the storm, the situation worsened. A new wind struck up. It was a strong southeasterly that pushed them the wrong direction entirely. If they'd had sails and a strong hull, they could have tacked across it and pressed on more quickly, but the gash in the hull that they had patched up was on the starboard side and left them vulnerable to the force of the new wind. To keep it sheltered from the worst of the waves, the ship had to be turned to the north, taking them farther off course.

From then on, the battle to survive was renewed in earnest. The ocean was nowhere near as violent as it had been in the storm, but the ship was now taking on more water than it had when it was simply drifting. The crew pumped and bailed around the clock, frantically trying to free themselves of the water that threatened to drag them down to the ocean floor. It was a battle with no end in sight.

Ten days after the storm, their rations were cut again. Captain Gother made another collection of outer garments to help plug the leaks, leaving the men wearing nothing but thin cotton shirts and trousers to protect them against the cold. The only way to get warm was to work at the pumps, but with so little food, nobody had the energy to exert themselves.

As each man felt weaker and weaker, they turned inward. Where there had been unity in the storm, with every man working as one, the crew of the *Greyhound* was now splintered and broken. Silence hung over the ship for hours on end, as each man retreated deeper into his own thoughts, deeper into his own fears.

Almost three weeks had passed since the storm when the first mate—a sinewy, leather-faced sailor named Richard Jackson with teeth the color of ship's timbers—told the captain that they would soon need to resort to eating human flesh if they were to survive.

The captain winced, checked that nobody else was nearby, and kept his voice low. "For the men to eat one of their own would be an abomination. We have enough provisions at the moment."

Jackson shrugged. "Well, I daresay this will not be the last time we discuss this. Some of the others are looking mighty weak. If we can't have enough men pumping, we'll all be feeding the sharks."

The conversation was over, but neither man moved.

"Perhaps," said the captain, "there is another way to change things."

"Yes?"

"We could rid ourselves of our Jonah."

"You think he's the reason for all this?" Jackson scoffed. "I never had you down as a man for fairy tales."

"Have you seen him when he's not at the pump? His head is always in the Bible, but I think he finds no peace in it. And at night he shouts, troubled by some terrible dream or other. Perhaps we would be better without his tormented soul on board."

From his position behind the water barrels, John had heard everything the men had said. Jackson's suggestion had not surprised him. He was sure that cannibalism had crossed the mind of every man on the *Greyhound* at some point. It was an open secret that this had happened on other ships in distress. But Captain Gother's comments about him were enough to leave him anxious and breathless, just like he had been before the storm.

The worst thing about the captain's words was that they were right. After the false sighting of land, it had become clear that their chances of survival were slim and dwindling further by the day. The chances of the *Greyhound* delivering them to safety were so low that death felt almost inevitable, and now there was talk of John himself being sacrificed for the sake of the crew. Would they really throw him overboard, believing he was the reason for their suffering? Would they eat him instead? It sounded so unthinkable, and yet the captain and Jackson had discussed it with all seriousness.

Faced with the fact that his life was in double jeopardy, John spent whatever time he was awake and not at the pump reading the Bible. At first he was looking for comfort, for a sign that all the sin he had committed might not send him straight to hell. The more he read—and the bleaker the outlook for the *Greyhound* became—the less sure he was about his eternal salvation.

He was just like the prodigal son. Having squandered everything and reached the lowest point possible, he was now determined to return home. Like the son in the parable as he turned his back on the pigsty and began the long journey back, he was unsure what would happen when he finally arrived. Would he be accepted, or would he be judged? Would he be welcomed, or would he be shunned? No matter how many times he read about the father running to greet his son and hosting a feast in honor of his return, John was unsure. Could he really expect God to welcome him back? Could someone like him be forgiven?

Somehow, the fear eased. With every day that passed and the *Greyhound* still remained afloat—and John not thrown overboard by the captain—the dread that troubled him lessened its grip. It was slow, like the task of pumping out the water from the hold, but the progress was clear. Day by day, he found that he could just about keep hope afloat.

So many questions remained about whether God would actually forgive him for his wretched ways, but he knew that they would have to wait. In the meantime, it was enough just to wake up in the morning and go to bed at night, thankful for another day. The longer death was kept at bay, the more he started to believe.

When the west coast of Ireland finally came into view, and the *Greyhound* limped into Lough Swilly, it was early April. Twenty-seven days had passed since the storm, and the ship was half-submerged and listing heavily on one side. Twenty-one months had passed since they set sail from England, and they had lost crew. Most of the little cargo they carried was ruined and the ship itself was so broken that it would take more than a month to patch it up so that it would be strong enough to make the brief crossing from the Irish sea to Liverpool.

The emaciated crew looked as weak as the battered ship. They had eaten the last handfuls of their salted cod and pig feed and drained the last of their water. What few clothes each man wore hung from his bones like rags, and they crept into Ireland looking more like prisoners of war than merchant sailors. There was relief etched across a few of their faces, but most bore the grim mask of the survivor. Having stared death in the face for twenty-seven long, uncertain days, life felt like a stranger.

John stood on the deck and watched the fishing boats make way to accommodate them as they progressed slowly up the narrow inlet. They had reached safe harbor at last. He returned the astonished stares, his own eyes just as wide, just as awed.

As the crew made fast the ship and dropped anchor, John noticed a presence beside him.

"Perhaps you were not our Jonah after all," said Captain Gother. "Perhaps you brought us good luck."

"No," said John. "Not I. There is a God who hears and answers prayers. That is why we are alive today. Not through our own strength, but his great mercy."

As soon as he could, John wrote to his father. Captain Newton had despaired of ever hearing from his son again, thinking he was lost forever. The letter arrived just days before the elder Newton would cross back over those same North Atlantic seas that nearly took John's life. Captain Newton was appointed to be the new governor of York Fort on Hudson's Bay, and if John had arrived back earlier he hoped his son might come with him.

Two years later, on a clear and calm summer day, Captain Newton drowned while out swimming in Hudson's Bay. It would be the father rather than the son who perished beneath the waves.

Richard Jackson had never considered himself to be a particularly ambitious man. Having been bred to the sea at age eleven and having spent the next twenty years in the service of Joseph Manesty, he had watched plenty of men fight for power. He could tell the first time he met them whether they were silver-tongued schemers who would take the credit for other people's work, or fighters who would scrap like a fighting cock to bring an opponent down. Regardless of the way they climbed, he had seen the way they placed all their hopes on the next promotion, on their first captaincy, on a bigger or better ship—only to find themselves hostage to fear of losing their status once they got there.

So, no, ambition was not for him. He knew his place. He had always thought of himself as more of a survivor than a climber, more rat or weasel than peacock or cockatoo. First mate on the *Greyhound* was as senior a position as a man like him could ever hope to reach. He had made his peace with it, even if it required him to put up with the repeated failings of the mutton-headed Captain Gother who sailed her. Not once had he spoken his mind, not once had he complained. He had simply kept his mouth shut and done his job.

And yet, when Richard Jackson—*Captain* Richard Jackson, no less—stood at the helm of the *Brownlow* and gave the order to cast off the lines and set sail for the Guinea coast, he allowed himself the briefest of smiles. He nodded farewell to Joseph Manesty on the quay, surveyed the docks of Liverpool as they slipped from view, and marveled at what was happening.

His voice, and his alone, was the one that the crew were listening to.

His voice, and his alone, had the power to move this fifty-eight-foot Guinea slaver away from the dock and out into the Irish Sea.

His voice, and his alone, was in charge.

He had never felt so important, so alive. Perhaps the pursuit of power wasn't so foolish after all. He leaned backward to fill his lungs with the stale dockside air and let out the cry that had been building within him for days.

"Here I have a hell of my own!"

It sounded less commanding than he had hoped, and he noticed that some of the crew looked at him strangely. No matter. He was the captain. He was in charge. This was his kingdom now.

Up until two weeks earlier, he hadn't dreamed that he would be given the command of the *Brownlow*. After the disaster of the *Greyhound*, he'd hardly expected to still be in Manesty's employment at all. He knew that Manesty wouldn't offer another ship to Captain Gother, for the fool had stayed far too long on the African coast, doing fundamental damage to the ship in the process. He suspected—feared, even—that he, too, might be stained by the *Greyhound*'s abject failure.

Then came the letter and the invitation to meet Manesty at his offices, where he had accepted the glass of Madeira wine to be polite, though he despised the sweet taste. He had listened carefully as Manesty had told him about the *Brownlow* and his plans to repair some of the damage to his accounts with a profitable run as a slaver. Manesty explained how lucrative a successful voyage could be, buying slaves in Africa for four to six pounds per head and selling them in the West Indies for ten times that amount. It was pleasant enough conversation, but Jackson spent most of it wondering what direction his employer was taking him.

"I offered the command to Newton," he said.

It was a surprising choice, but a logical one. Captain Newton was well-known among the trade, and broadly respected too. "So the captain is no longer with the Royal African Company?"

"Not that Newton. I mean his son, John. The one you brought back from the Guinea coast."

Jackson was stunned and momentarily thrown off guard. But a lifetime at sea had taught him to be prepared for sudden change. There was no point in wasting time asking why. Better to decide what to do about it. "He has knowledge of the trade," Jackson mused. "And experience at sea. I can understand—"

Manesty was not finished and waved his glass, signaling Jackson to stop. "He said no. He said he would rather serve as first mate on his first voyage in the Guinea trade before taking command of the next."

"I see." Jackson inhaled deeply, taking in the sweet aroma of the wine. In all his years at sea, he had never encountered anyone willing to use feigned humility like this as a foil for vaulting ambition. Surely that was what Newton was doing. It was bold. And foolish.

"Which leaves me in need of a captain," Manesty continued. "Are you willing?"

Jackson replayed the conversation countless times after leaving Manesty's office, letting the memory warm him throughout the busy two weeks that led up to their departure. But as the departure approached and he moved his sea chest into the *Brownlow*'s captain's cabin and prepared to greet the crew, something began to trouble him.

It was Newton. Specifically, which version of John Newton was going to join him as first mate?

Would it be the wild-eyed, barefoot man grown black whom they had first met at Kittam?

Or might it be the hard-drinking, profanity-spewing singer of bawdy songs that had sailed with them up and down the Guinea coast?

Could it be the tortured, nervous slip of a man who had seemed to unravel like a torn sail as they approached the Grand Banks of Newfoundland?

Or would it be the pious, Bible-reading man who spent hours at church when the rest of the crew were helping with repairs at Lough Swilly?

Jackson hoped to God that it would be the first or the second. However, the moment that Newton strode onto the deck and greeted his captain warmly, mumbling some inane nonsense about being grateful for God's blessing and praying for his protection, Jackson knew that the months ahead had just become a good deal more challenging.

"So, Newton," he said as the last trace of the English coast disappeared from view. "You chose not to stay at home and enjoy your inheritance. The lure of the Guinea coast and all her delights was too strong, eh? You can do what you want when we get there, just as long as you disappear off into the jungle."

Newton didn't react. He just kept his eyes fixed on the horizon and held the silence for the longest time. "There was no inheritance," he said eventually. "It was just a lie of Captain Gother's to persuade me to return."

Jackson pondered his next move. If Newton knew about Gother's lie, he would have suspected that Jackson was in on it as well. That could be a problem. "You are not angry?"

"Not at all. I returned home to a far greater reward than £400 a year."

He tried to suppress his sneer. "You did? Must have been some reward to surpass a fortune like that."

"I am to be married," Newton said. "Upon the successful completion of our trade here, I shall be in a position to wed. It has all been agreed between our two families."

"So you are here because of your ambitions. I understand."

Newton inhaled as if he was about to reply but said nothing. Jackson turned and studied him properly for the first time. He had never realized what a strange-looking fellow Newton was. He was twenty-three years old, but his skin was weathered, scarred, and worn, just like a sailor who had long since retired from the sea. His eyes were soft and innocent, as if he was expecting only good things in life, but his mouth was small, tense, guarded. It turned up a little, as if he was permanently remembering some sour taste he hoped to avoid.

"Well, whatever you do, Newton, just make sure you don't return home with the pox. Young brides can be funny about that."

Newton recoiled. "I have no intention whatsoever of . . . that. I love her. I want to serve her as Christ serves the church."

Jackson didn't bother trying to hide his sneer. The last thing Jackson wanted was to have a first mate who hid himself away from the men like some kind of monk, but that was precisely what he had got. The worst Newton of all had joined him on the *Brownlow*, one who would only make the role of captain more difficult for Jackson. If the voyage was to be a success at all, it would be in spite of Newton, not because of him.

But perhaps there was good news buried within this revelation as well. If Newton really was going to continue to live as a God-fearing, clean-mouthed disciple, there was no future for him at all in the trade. This was a business for hardened men, not saints. As long as Jackson turned a profit on the *Brownlow*, his future looked bright.

John climbed back on board the shallop, made doubly sure that his cargo was held fast, and gave the order to return to the ship. He closed his eyes for a moment, breathing slow and deep. He tried hard to ignore both the persistent rain and the fear of what would happen when he returned and faced Captain Jackson again.

A memory returned to him. He was sitting in the office of Joseph Manesty, an untouched glass of wine to the side. Manesty had just offered him the captaincy of the *Brownlow*. He wanted to say yes but knew he had to say no.

"Until now I have been unsettled and careless. I think I had better take another voyage first and learn to obey."

How naive he had been.

As first mate, his main duty while on the Guinea coast was trading. Each time the *Brownlow* neared a factory—either those on the coast that advertised their stock with smoke signals or the others that could only be found after days and days of rowing inland—Captain Jackson ordered the anchor dropped and the shallop prepared. John would select his half dozen men, order someone to check that the leg irons, neck collars, and assorted chains were all in place and in good condition, check them himself, then set out.

It was nothing new to John. His months spent working in Kittam had taught him everything he would ever need to know about the trade. He knew all the ways in which traders like him were tricked and cheated. He knew how to spot when he was being lied to, and he knew when not to challenge those lies. There was no man on board the *Brownlow* more qualified to trade than him. And yet, it felt nothing like it did when he was in Kittam. He took no pleasure in his work.

There were some clear reasons why. One was the fact that men were dying. Already two of his crew had drowned when the shallop capsized while trying to reach land. Several more had perished at the hands of a fever that struck when they were four days upriver. As first mate, John was responsible for the safety of his crew. He had a duty to care for his men, yet he was powerless to save them.

Then there was Captain Jackson. From the moment they left Liverpool, he had treated John with disdain. He had constantly reminded John that when they reached the Guinea coast and began their work, he must follow his captain's orders. He told John that managing a factory in Kittam was very different to being first mate on board a slaver. He said there was no room for weakness.

Jackson wasted no time demonstrating his lesson.

As soon as the barricado was in place and the nets around the gunnel had been erected, Jackson had made a habit of throwing offal and other animal waste into the sea. Within a day or two there were sharks circling the boat, eager and expectant. John had seen a few sharks while he was on the *Levant*, but nobody ever paid them much attention. Captain Jackson, however, welcomed them like old friends, knowing the terror they would strike in everyone on board. He would stand on the deck and hurl the ship's waste to them, laughing and cheering as they churned the water white.

The journey back from the coastal factory to the *Brownlow* was quick, and John was on board before the sharks could turn their attention to the shallop.

Captain Jackson was waiting for him on deck with the rest of the crew. They were all armed. The ship's slaves were there also, all those for whom Newton had bartered earlier—twenty-four males—chained in pairs, standing behind the barricado—thirteen females, and six children standing free on deck.

"Line them up," Jackson said, rubbing his hands together as the crew dragged the three new slaves into a line.

Nobody spoke.

Captain Jackson moved slowly, examining each one thoroughly in turn. Teeth and mouth. Eyes and ears. He prodded their arms and thighs, slapping hard to check the quality of the muscle. They were exceptional, yet John knew there would be no praise from the captain.

"No females?"

"No," said John. "They were weak."

"Hmm. And how much?"

John said the price.

Captain Jackson twitched. "Each?"

"For all three." It was a better price than any other trader could have hoped for.

The silence continued as Captain Jackson wrote down brief descriptions of numbers twenty-five, twenty-six, and twenty-seven in his log.

When he was finished, John nodded at one of the crew to take them through the barricado. He was looking forward to returning to his cabin and trying again to write to Polly.

"Wait," said Captain Jackson. "I should like them to see this. And the others too."

He looked over toward a crewmember standing near his cabin and told him to bring her out.

Everyone on the ship watched the man disappear from view before re-emerging, shuffling backward. A dull *thud* echoed as he dragged the lifeless body onto the deck. John shifted to get a better look. He recognized her instantly. He had bought number nine the previous week from a trader far upriver. She had been perfectly well when he brought her on board.

John looked at Captain Jackson, wondering whether he was going to blame him for the death. "What happened?"

"Died this morning. Just a fever," he said, breezily. Turning to the crew and the rest of the faces staring down at their feet, he filled his lungs and prepared to bellow for all to hear.

"There is a common belief in these parts that when they die, they will return to their homeland." He paused, a wry smile creeping onto his lips. "They say that they will *go to their happy country*. Number nine here died of natural causes, but some of them are so keen to return to their happy country that they will gladly kill themselves to hasten that journey. Obviously, that is bad for our business."

Silence.

"Now, we have the nets and the barricado and the men are in chains, but I have always considered myself to be a thorough person. I do not like the thought of losing any of our profits and I have no time for fools who believe in fantasies."

He paused for a moment to direct another crew member to untie a section of the netting on the port side of the ship. John felt his heart start to race.

"Gather round," Captain Jackson called as he stepped forward and helped to lift the body up onto the gunnel. "I believe that it is my duty as captain to do what I can to disabuse these beasts from their ridiculous notions. We don't want them to believe that death offers the promise of escape. We don't want them to look forward to the moment that they die. We want them to be terrified of it!"

With that, he hauled the body over. It hit the water. Nobody moved.

"Men, make sure they all watch this, you here?"

The crew waved their pistols and corralled everyone to port. Nobody disobeyed. Everybody stared at the water and the naked body floating on the surface.

"Ah," said Captain Jackson, a broad smile on his face. "Look at that."

The sharks arrived. Four of them. They were cautious at first, circling the body, then prodding at it with their snouts. As soon as one of them took the first bite, the others joined in. The sharks thrashed with ten times the violence they usually displayed when the captain fed them mere scraps.

On the deck they could see the water instantly stained red. Hear the sound of limbs being torn apart. See the sharks' eyes rolling back and their teeth bared as they took bite after bite.

John glanced at Captain Jackson. He was not looking at the water. Instead, he was staring at the slaves. His eyes were shark-wide, teeth bared as he inhaled deeply once again.

"This is not your happy country!" he shouted, his fingers jabbing at the silent men and women. Most of them avoided his gaze. Some were still transfixed on the carnage in the water below. "This is my ship, do you hear? And on it I have created a hell of my own!"

Something else was troubling John more than Captain Jackson's cruelty or the weight of responsibility for the men under his command. He had boarded the *Brownlow* with the best intentions. He vowed that he would live as a strong Christian, praying multiple times a day, refraining from all vices, and refusing even a moment of idleness. He was determined to fill every spare moment with the study of Scripture and deep reflection on God's mercies.

He lasted one day. Maybe two.

The farther they had sailed from England, the more he had struggled. By the time the Guinea coast came into view, his Bible was buried deep in his sea chest and his plans for spiritual discipline were little more than a hazy memory. He was powerless to resist the temptations on offer.

Back in the frozen North Atlantic, where death loomed daily and his life was in the greatest peril he had ever known, he found it easy to study and pray and live right. He had wanted to do it. Now, when life had never been easier, righteous living held no appeal. He had lost all desire to be a man of strong faith.

He berated himself at first. He tried to summon the strength to recover his virtues. It was little use. His armor was gone, his defenses overrun. Vices won out. He was like Samson, a man once convinced of his own strength now humbled by his weakness and trapped by his enemies. The longer they sailed, the more he felt as though he was in chains again.

Captain Jackson was delighted.

"You look like your old self again," he would say from time to time, his forced smile revealing his mouthful of mahogany-brown teeth.

Clapping a heavy hand on John's back, he might comment, "I like a man who knows how to have a little sport, Mr. Newton. And I can tell from the glint in your eye that you feel the same. There's plenty of fun to be had on a Guinea slaver. We'll make it a hell for the cargo, but there's no reason why we can't make it a heaven for you and I."

Yet Captain Jackson's worst comment—the one that robbed John of sleep for nights to come—was said as innocently as a dove.

"There," he said one morning, pointing to a small island that had been marked on the map. "Plantain Island. Rumor has it there's a trader called Evans that set up a factory there. Sells the best stock for a hundred miles. You can take the shallop and one man to Evans while the *Brownlow* stays moored here in Pirate Bay at Sierra Leone. The lads need some fun here."

By the time John and his man dropped anchor and waded through the shallows at Plantain Island, he was desperate. He had barely slept in five nights. His head felt like it was gripped by one of the slave collars. His mind was racing constantly and peace was a distant memory.

If P. I. was surprised to see him, she did not show it. She greeted him as though they had never met. Evidently, Evans had died. But she and the others with her were courteous and welcoming, inviting him to take a drink with them after a stroll along the lime-tree avenue.

"They will bear fruit next year," said P. I. "Such a lot has changed."

"Yes," said John. "A great many things."

If John had been feeling better, he might have taken this as his cue to remind her of his previous time on the island. He was starting to feel faint and nauseous, and it took all his strength and concentration just to keep himself upright.

Eventually, when their first meeting was over, John was able to excuse himself and return to his lodging on the island. He just made it to the cabin before collapsing, exhausted and shivering, cold sweats breaking on his brow.

The fever grew worse throughout the night. John lay, halfway between sleep and wakefulness, the minutes edging by like hours. Vivid images imposed themselves on his mind—memories of all the ways in which he had failed to live up to his standards. He remembered the storm on the *Greyhound*, the fear that was written on every face but his. He recalled how it drove him to prayer, how he was sure that God was the only one who could save them, only to relapse once life was easy again. He began to wish that he had sunk to the ocean floor when he had first cried out to God. Better to die calling for mercy than live mired in sin.

He lay still, the terrible truth slowly breaking over him. The door of hope was shut. Nothing could save him now.

His heart was racing so fast that lying in his bed was impossible. He slipped out of the cabin and into the night. The moon was full and bright, and he stood a while watching the shadows it cast on the trees at the edge of the island.

He knew those trees well. They had offered him shelter many times. It was there among them that the visiting trader had found him.

John could barely walk. He half crawled through the trees to a quiet spot on the beach. When he reached the dry sand, he collapsed on his knees and began to pray.

At first there were no words. Only deep, shuddering sobs and heavy tears.

He could make no more grand resolutions.

No more wild promises.

All he could do was surrender.

"I am a wretched sinner," he said eventually, tears falling onto his open hands. "Do with me as you please."

Two days after he stumbled onto that lonely beach on Plantain Island, John was back on board the *Brownlow*. He answered Captain Jackson's questions about the slaves he had bought from P. I., then disappeared to his cabin. Something was different within him. The Atlantic storm that had nearly swallowed the *Greyhound* had marked a turning point in his life, the moment when his conscience was finally awakened. But his fever on Plantain Island felt even more dramatic, even more significant. It was the moment when John finally placed his trust in the cross of Christ. It was the point when he finally realized that he needed God to do for him what he could not do for himself. He was a wretch, and he needed grace. His fever was gone too. It disappeared almost as soon as he surrendered himself to God.

Life continued more simply and quietly for John for the rest of their time on the Guinea coast. He carried out his duties as first mate, making long journeys upstream and others inland on foot in pursuit of trade. Some of his men fell ill, and he was constantly on his guard. He endured wind, rain, and storm in the shallop, his old maladies flaring up as a result. More than once or twice he was capsized in the treacherous waters around the shore and was dragged, half dead, to safety. Danger and discomfort were his constant companions, and he was grateful for them both. Like ropes that tether a ship to the dock, they kept him close to God.

When the *Brownlow* had been trading for eight months, Captain Jackson declared to John at dinner that they had enough stock to sail to the West Indies. They had a cargo of 218 men, women, and children, and conditions in the hold were so cramped that there was a danger of disease and death eating into their profits. It was time to sail and time to sell.

John was relieved. Leaving Africa meant that he would be home within months. He would have a share of healthy profits and the opportunity to take command of his own Guinea trader for Mr. Manesty. Finally, he would marry Polly. Finally, his life would begin.

There was one last job that John had to attend to before they sailed west. The ship needed to be resupplied with firewood and drinking water, and it was up to the first mate to make multiple trips to a trading post a short way upriver. John fell into an easy rhythm, making his trip in the afternoon when the sea breeze was behind him, loading up in the evening, then returning in the morning with the land wind filling the shallop's sails.

He was about to untether from the *Brownlow* and make one of his last trips inland when Captain Jackson called out from the deck.

"Mr. Newton, a word in my cabin, please."

John looked up. The shallop was old and temperamental, and he didn't like to miss the good wind that would take him to the river. Still, he hid his frustration and climbed back on board and found Captain Jackson in his cabin.

"You have some further orders for me, Captain?"

Captain Jackson appeared distracted, staring into the middle distance. "No, Newton. But . . . I took it in my head that you should remain on the ship today."

"Why? I have made every other trip."

"I know. But not this one. Send someone else."

John swallowed his complaint, left the cabin to instruct a replacement, and watched the shallop sail in the late afternoon sun. It was a strange situation that made no sense to him, yet he had no appetite for a fight over it. Captain Jackson had proven himself to be a ruthless, even brutal commander. There was little to be gained from irritating him.

The next morning John watched a small vessel approach. It wasn't the shallop, and it contained no water, no timber, and none of the crew from the *Brownlow*. It was a canoe, paddled by the man he had been buying timber from.

The canoe pulled level and the man shouted up to John.

"Your shallop," he called. "It sank. Last night at the river. Your man is dead."

It was a shock to the whole crew, especially Captain Jackson.

"I do not know why I stopped you from going," he said when they were alone in his cabin. "I just had it in my mind that you should stay here. Why would that happen, Newton? Was it God?"

John smiled. "I believe so. Many are the dangers he guides us through."

For several days Captain Jackson continued to be affected by the event. John noticed that he was quieter and less prone to his typical outbursts, but it was not a permanent transformation. As they set out on the Middle Passage, conditions on board started to deteriorate. Sickness swept through the hold and soon there were deaths. Captain Jackson ordered the bodies thrown to the sharks that were still patiently tracking the *Brownlow*. Unlike with the first body he had fed them, he did not order everyone on board to watch. There was no delight on his face either. Just the pain of a man seeing his profits churn to blood in the waters below.

The slaves rebelled at their conditions. There were fights below deck almost every night as men, chained in pairs, struggled to reach the buckets that served as latrines, then battled to be the farthest away from them when they spilled in rough seas. The fighting carried over into the daytime, and extra sailors were posted on the barricado, their guns always primed and ready to shoot. There were rumors of attempted insurrections and plots among the males to kill all the crew. When Captain Jackson discovered the identity of the leaders, he wanted nothing more than to feed them to the sharks, alive. Instead, he thought of the profits and placed them in thumbscrews for days on end.

By the time they reached their final destination of Charleston, South Carolina, sixty-two of the slaves had died.

For John, the numbers did not cause much trouble. He wanted a profit as much as Captain Jackson did, but with just eight weeks' sailing between them and Liverpool, all John could think about was Polly.

Finally, seven years after they had first met, they would be married.

It was tantalizingly close. Once Captain Jackson had sold the last of the slaves, purchased whatever rum, tobacco, or cotton he could get, and overseen the transformation of the *Brownlow* from a floating slave prison to merchant trader, they would finally be on their way.

It took weeks. While the crew whored and drank their nights away in Charleston, John wandered in the woods when he could, seeking peace and an escape from temptation. When he was forced to join them in whatever tavern they had chosen, he held fast to his determination.

"I am a spectator," he reminded himself, over and over. "Not a sharer in their pleasures."

It was part prayer, part promise. A declaration of intent as much as a plea for help.

Chapter 8 —————— Shackles (1750-1754)

Captain John Newton sat in the cabin of the *Duke of Argyle* and penned another letter to his wife. It was nine months to the day since their wedding in February, twelve weeks since he had sailed from Liverpool, and ten days since the ship arrived on the Guinea coast and commenced trading. He wrote two or three times a week, yet never struggled to fill the blank pages. Every time he closed the cabin door and sat down to write, the words came as easily as if Polly were sitting right there with him.

Despite the fact that he would be unable to post his stack of letters until he met another ship that was heading back to England, he took delight in describing the details of life on board. The voyage would keep them apart for more than a year, and his letter-writing became an important ritual. It was his way of keeping her in his thoughts, of holding her close.

He didn't tell her everything, of course. Some details of the trade were not suitable to share with a wife. So while he told her about the *Duke of Argyle* being a twenty-year-old, one-hundred-ton, double-masted snow with ten cannon on board, he did not dwell on the adjustments they had made to prepare her for the trade. In previous letters he had mentioned the barricado, but not the six guns he had ordered placed along the top to instill fear in the slaves in the hope it might deter them from rebelling. He had told her about the hard work of the carpenter, but not the two-foot-four-inch headroom that the male captives would have to endure down in the hold. She knew that Manesty had instructed him to buy 250 slaves, but not how many deaths along the route he and Manesty had factored in as the cost of doing business. She knew that he would spend several months trading along the west coast of Africa, but nothing about the sharks.

As much as the ship itself needed attention, the crew demanded even more of his time. In previous letters he had described those under his command in vague detail. He had explained that there were twenty-nine of them, including a cook, a surgeon, and three apprentice boys. He talked about setting watches and preparing them all for the challenge of trading, securing, and keeping alive so many slaves for so many months. He had not told her how many of his men were jailbirds, runaways, or already ruined by alcohol. He hadn't mentioned which men he had already decided were most likely to lead a mutiny.

Today, John was in a wholly positive mood. The first leg of the journey from Liverpool had been a success. He had worked hard to establish his authority, and there were already signs that he had earned the men's respect. He was feeling good, and he wanted Polly to know that he was making a success of his job.

He started the letter with the usual greetings, then moved on to the topic of the crew.

> *If I say to one, Come, he comes; if to another, Go, he flies. If I order one person to do something, perhaps three or four will be ambitious . . .*

He paused. Serving as first mate on the *Brownlow* had taught many important lessons. Even Richard Jackson—cruel, aggressive, and unpredictable as he was—had given John an example to follow. John had observed in him the way a captain should behave toward his crew, expecting total obedience and respect.

> *Not a man in the ship must eat his dinner till I please to give him leave. . . . There is a mighty business of attendance when I leave the ship, and a strict watch kept when I am absent, lest I should return unawares.*

He read back what he had written and decided it needed explaining. The last thing he wanted was for Polly to think he was getting drunk on power.

> *I would have you judge from my manner of relating to these ceremonials, that I do not value them highly for their own sake; but they are old established customs, and necessary to be kept up; for, without a strict discipline, the common sailors would be unmanageable.*

His mind drifted, imagining how bad things could get on ship. All his life he had heard cautionary tales of weak or foolish men struggling to control a mutinous crew. Some of those captains paid with their lives. Some of the crew whose attempts at mutiny failed had found themselves on Execution Dock, paying for their crimes with their lives as well.

Within a month of their arrival on the Guinea coast, John observed among the crew the first signs of dissent. It started when three men were sent to the coast for business. When they returned to the ship—bruised, bloodied, and a long way from sober—John wondered about punishing them, but decided against it. It took less than twenty-four hours for him to regret his leniency. The loudest of the group, a common sailor named William Lees, refused to perform his duties.

"But it's Captain Newton's orders," he was told.

He laughed. "Newton? I swear I'll not serve that man."

John felt that he had no choice but to have him whipped, put in irons, and chained on deck until he begged to be released.

Lees lasted three days.

The crew were not the only source of tension. Trading itself was difficult. Up and down the Guinea coast they heard the same story—wars between tribes were raging inland, and there were far fewer slaves coming through to the traders on the coast. John's first mate regularly returned to the *Argyle* empty-handed, or with nothing but children. John had never really liked buying children; somehow it seemed wrong to him.

The weeks passed and their numbers remained low. Reaching 250 slaves was a tall order at the best of times, but at this rate, it would take them the best part of a year. John had no intention of letting the *Duke of Argyle* stew in the equatorial humidity for so long and run the risk of ending up like the *Greyhound*.

John planned to finish trading in May, seven months after they first arrived on the Guinea coast. The closer the deadline, the more desperate he became. So when he heard about a trader who was selling a batch of twenty slaves—slaves that he knew had already rebelled once and overtaken a French slaver before being recaptured and sold again—John ignored the risks and accepted the trade. He increased the number of armed guards on deck at all times, re-spiked the barricado, and made sure that all weapons were regularly cleaned and reloaded. He also declared that when the slaves were allowed on deck to be fed, the guards should regularly fire into the air to deter them from considering rebellion. It was a detail that he chose not to include in one of his letters to Polly.

The slaves themselves were a source of concern. John could tell they were restless. Each morning when they were brought up for feeding and airing, he noticed many of them were bleeding. Their bodies were rubbed raw by the chains at their ankles and the rough wooden planks in the hold. It bothered him to see them emerge like this, but it worried him more when he heard shouting from the hold below. Most of the time it meant that one of the men was unable to climb up on deck because the man chained to him had died. John would order the body thrown overboard, though he never made anybody watch the sharks as they thrashed below. He had no desire to emulate Captain Jackson in that regard.

As their time on the coast came to an end, the situation worsened. Trading had been slow and difficult, and John was forced to abandon all hope of reaching his goal of 250 slaves. The weather was even more brutal than usual, with scorching days and damp, foggy nights. The hold where the men slaves were kept became unbearable for the crewmen who carried out the weekly inspections while the men were up on deck. They complained that the air was so hot and the odor so foul they could not breathe. Yet John was in no mood to stop the hold inspections, especially when they found two knives hidden there.

William Lees continued to cause trouble. He tried to hide on shore one day, hoping that John would simply forget about him and sail away. It cost John a whole gallon of brandy to persuade some local natives to chain Lees and bring him back to the ship.

All day long John sweated and battled to find the energy to carry out his tasks. It was a struggle just to breathe and move, let alone keep the ship safe and try to trade. Again, John found comfort in his cabin, writing long letters to Polly or adding to the ship's log. He wrote about Lees, who attacked some traders when they came on board and earned himself another spell in chains on the deck. Later, when John saw a British naval warship anchored nearby, John wasted no time trading William Lees and two more crewmen for men the navy wanted rid of.

It was not the end of the ship's problems either. A bout of sickness was spreading throughout the ship. On December 18, 1750, crewman Lawson died. "Ill with a fever," John wrote in his ship's log. "Was obliged to bury him immediately, being extremely offensive."

January 20, 1751, marked the death of John Birdson, "after sustaining the most violent fever I have ever seen 3 days."

It wasn't just crew who were dying. Earlier, on January 9, John recorded that he "buried a fine woman slave. No. 11, having been ailing some time." Then slave number 27 died on February 3 ("very bad with a flux"), while on February 13 he "buried a boy slave (No. 66), who was taken ill with a violent flux." Flux, with its bloody diarrhea, was a brutal killer that spread throughout the ship at will. John wondered if it would ever stop. On February 23, John "buried a man slave (No. 33), having been a fortnight ill of a flux, which has baffled all our medicines." Again on Sunday, April 21, there was more death to register: "We have almost every day one or more taken with a flux, of which a woman died to night (No. 79)."

Death had taken hold of the *Duke of Argyle*. It appeared reluctant to let go.

At last, some good news. The sickness that hung like a fog over the ship lifted long enough for them to stock up on timber and water and prepare to set sail for Antigua at the end of May. The *Duke of Argyle* carried nothing like the 250 that Manesty had called for. Instead, it carried just 156 slaves. Yet with the trade winds at their backs and the slowest part of the voyage now behind them, John felt a little of his original optimism return. Given the poor trading conditions on the coast and the illness, 156 was not a bad number. Manesty was a reasonable man and John was confident that he would understand and give him another ship to command. Next time he would do better, he was sure of it.

On some days during their sprint across the Atlantic, it was difficult to get the slaves up to get fresh air on deck. They were not like experienced sail-ors, and if the waves were high, then no amount of gunshot in the air could get them to move. Many days it was just too cold. But John insisted that all the men be brought out from the hold as often as possible. Conditions below were deteriorating, and death among the slaves was becoming increasingly common.

One day, when they were a little more than halfway to Antigua, John was woken by shouting. Raised voices were nothing unusual on any Guinea trader that was carrying slaves. If it wasn't the crew trying to issue orders, it was the slaves themselves fighting down below. But on this occasion, the urgency of the voices was impossible to ignore. John leaped from his bed and ran out to the deck, half-dressed.

He found the doorway in the barricado open and five of the crew on the other side, pointing their weapons at a group of twenty slaves. John recognized them instantly as the men who had overrun the French trader. None of them were wearing leg irons or chains.

"They broke free," said the gunner, sweat falling in his eyes, chest heaving, holding a foot-long thick metal spike in his free hand. "I thought I heard a commotion down there and we went to investigate. I found this marlinespike among 'em. They must have used it to break free."

It was a near miss, and John spent much of the rest of the morning wonder-ing what would have happened if the gunner hadn't caught them when he did. Another hour or more and so many slaves would have been freed that they would easily have overrun the crew.

By the afternoon his men had identified the six ringleaders.

"What do you want to do with them?" the gunner asked.

John knew full well what Captain Jackson would have done. It would have been bloody, brutal, and resulted in the immediate crossing out of six more numbers in the ship's inventory. He thought he knew, too, what Captain Phelps of the *Levant* would have done, most likely letting them go with a light punishment. Neither particularly appealed to John. They both were too extreme. He wanted a different option, something that would still act as a deterrent but not harm his profits.

"Thumbscrews," he announced carefully. "Chain them up on the deck so everyone can see them. Two days should do it. Perhaps three."

John was right. There were no more rebellions from that moment on. But there were more deaths. A lot more deaths. Sickness returned, sweeping over the ship like waves over the *Greyhound*. Those who survived looked like mere shadows of the men, women, and children whom John had bought in Africa not long since and then imprisoned below deck. The ship's cargo was made up of living, breathing humans, but they moved more like ghosts.

As they reached Antigua, John ordered the crew to prepare for the scramble—a frantic practice where prospective buyers would rush aboard the ship soon after it docked and buy up the slaves that were lined up on deck. First, they readied the slaves. The crew shaved heads, oiled bodies to give the appearance of a lustrous shine, and did what they could to disguise the welts and open wounds. Next, they turned to the ship. Thick canvas sails were strung up over the main deck like a tent, transforming it into a shaded, gloomy space that hid the worst of the slaves' sores. The slaves were then arranged in rows on deck and the signal given to the waiting buyers.

The scramble was wild, as John knew it would be. He stood to the side as buyers charged around the deck, eyes frantically scanning the bodies for those they wanted, elbowing their way forward when they found one who looked promising. They threw chains made of rope over the necks of the ones they liked, then hurried off in search of another bargain.

For the slaves themselves, it was terrifying. They were left deliberately clueless, as fear made most of them meek. A few might try to break through any gaps in the canvas and throw themselves overboard in hope of escape, but the crew were armed and ready. For the most part, the cries were muted.

When each trader was finished, the scramble entered its darkest moment. Purchased slaves were hurried off the *Duke of Argyle* and loaded into small boats. The new owners knew nothing and cared even less about the past lives of their purchases. Relationships that had formed and grown in the months the slaves had been on board were suddenly ripped apart. Husbands were torn from wives. Children torn from parents. Muffled tears gave way to screams. The air was loud with the polyglot cries of many different African languages and dialects, as shrieking, sobbing slaves were thrust deeper into hell. The Middle Passage had been bad enough. But entering the bloody maw of the plantation system in the West Indies, one third of them would be dead within three years.

When their business was finally over in Antigua and they had begun the seven-week voyage home, John sat in his cabin and wrote up the accounts. The scramble had been a success. John had sold everything he arrived with, as he knew he would. But the losses had been great. Of the 156 slaves they had left Africa with, 10 had died on the Middle Passage. Plus the loss of the 18 who died before leaving the Guinea coast. It was a much higher level of loss than he had hoped for. He stared at the figures on the page. There was no way of hiding the damage the death had inflicted on the profits.

He kept on writing, for there was another set of numbers that troubled John even more. Of the twenty-nine crew he had left Liverpool with, seven had died. To lose so many slaves was bad for business. To lose so many crew was bad for his soul.

The accounts finished, he thought about writing to Polly. For once, he had nothing to say.

After returning, John was able to spend eight months at home with Polly. But then John's second voyage as captain began. His new command was another double-masted snow with a carrying capacity of 250 slaves, just like the *Duke of Argyle*. Yet the *African* was different in one key regard—it was brand-new, and this was to be her maiden voyage. Having returned the *Duke of Argyle* in one piece but without a profit, John embraced the fresh start that the *African* offered. He was determined to do things differently this time and retained only two crewmen from his previous voyage.

John departed Liverpool at the end of June 1752 with a clear plan for how to manage the crew on the voyage. His main aim was to stamp out the worst of their vices and encourage them to turn their attention to higher pursuits. There was no fiddler on board, but he had brought a well-stocked library, ready to educate the men by the study of Latin, French, the classics, and mathematics.

He held mandatory prayers twice on Sundays and insisted that the crew join him in observing the Sabbath.

His Bible was now accompanied by a spiritual diary. He wrote in it daily, keeping constant track of his efforts and successes, of his hopes for the voyage ahead and the lessons learned along the way. In the opening pages, he recorded his purpose: "to bring myself a deep sense of my past sins and follies," "to enlarge my mind," and "to compose my heart to a perfect peace & charity with all mankind." Indeed, John hoped to be "a good soldier under the banner of Jesus Christ."

From the very start, John felt encouraged. The men showed up on Sundays, listened to their captain's homilies, and appeared to be uttering fewer profanities and blasphemies. Even the weather itself was on their side, with just one brief storm slowing their progress to the Guinea coast. As the coast of Sierra Leone came into view, John retreated to his cabin, reflected on the state of affairs on the *African*, and happily wrote to Mary of the ship as his "peaceful kingdom."

He was wrong.

Five months into the voyage, he was visited by crewman William Cooney. He was careful to close the cabin door and kept his voice low as he addressed his captain.

"It's Swain, sir. He asked me to sign a round-robin."

John was dumbstruck and needed a moment to process the news. A round-robin was a declaration of mutinous intent written in a box in the middle of a piece of paper. As the paper was passed around the crew, those that were willing to lend their support to the overthrow of the captain signed their names around the outside, like petals on a daisy. That way, it was impossible to tell who had signed first or who was really behind the mutiny. A round-robin was about as serious a problem as any captain would ever face.

"I . . . I thought myself very secure from any danger of this kind," John said.

"As did I, Captain."

"Everybody has behaved very quiet the whole voyage."

"They have, Captain."

"I do not remember the least complaint or grievance."

Cooney shifted awkwardly and remained silent.

"You will find out who is behind this and tell me?"

"I will, Captain."

For days, John was in suspense. Cooney could not uncover the identity of the men behind the round-robin, and John was left wondering. He studied the crew carefully, trying to discern which ones might be against him and which ones for him, but it was impossible to tell for sure.

It took another sailor to uncover the truth and inform John. There were three men at the heart of the rebellion—Swain, Forrester, and Mackdonald. They had spent weeks trying to recruit others to their side and had even begun openly sharing their plan to kill or seriously wound the ship's doctor.

As John discovered the identities of the plotters, the ship was hit hard with illness. Mackdonald died of a sudden fever, but Swain and Forrester were well enough to be chained at the ankle and at the wrist. Within a month John handed them over to the *Earl of Halifax*, a passing trader, with the instruction to transfer them onto the first navy warship they met. The troublemakers were gone.

John was grateful that the affair was over and the crisis averted. It seemed to him as though God himself had intervened, saving the ship from certain disaster and allowing them to continue to trade in peace.

The relief did not last long. Not long after Swain and Forrester had been sent off, John was inspecting the male quarters below deck when he saw two slaves trying to remove their irons. Further searches revealed knives, stones, shot, and a chisel, tools with which the slaves could easily have broken their chains and overrun the crew.

John had a clear idea where the tools came from and how they ended up below deck, and so he ordered the young boy slaves who had the run of the ship and were never chained to be rounded up and questioned. He was careful to only use the thumbscrews lightly on such fragile hands, and the pain was enough to encourage them to identify the six rebel leaders among the men. The six were duly punished, with four being placed in iron collars, which made it almost impossible for them to rest and recover from their wounds. Like Swain and Forrester, they, too, were sent to the *Earl of Halifax*.

"O my soul praise the Lord," John wrote in his spiritual diary when the rebels were finally gone. God was his "always gracious preserver." Knowing how precarious his life was, he prayed also to be ready to die trusting only in his Redeemer.

The relief he felt was interrupted, however, the day that William Cooney—the same man who had saved the ship and possibly John's life by reporting the round-robin—raped a female slave in full view of the rest of the crew and most of the slaves.

John ordered Cooney placed in irons, but the matter was not so easy to deal with. The woman, Number 83, was heavily pregnant. "If anything happens to the woman I shall impute it to him, for she was big with child," he wrote in his diary. "I hope this has been the first affair of the kind on board and I am determined to keep them quiet if possible."

Somehow, despite the plotted rebellion and the public rape, a peace soon settled on the *African*. The slaves were subdued, calm even. Trading was good, and as they approached eight months on the coast, they carried more than two hundred slaves. But John was no fool, and he continued to guard all of them closely. His faith led him to trust God to play his part, and he held fast to the words of Psalm 127: "Except the LORD keep the city, the watchman waketh but in vain" (v. 1).

When John took his place on deck while the slaves were eating, surveying the men, women, and children that he had bought and held captive on his ship, he could only rest content and thank God. To his eyes, as he looked at men in leg chains, women fearful of rape, and children taken from their families, it looked like a peaceful, happy scene. He was so certain of this he made a point to write that they were "more like children in one family, than slaves in iron and chains."

Knowing how many slaves to take on board, how long to trade before leaving Africa, and when to attempt the Middle Passage—everyone in the business knew that it was a gamble. On ships running at full capacity, conditions were appalling. The slaves—lying in two rows, one above the other, on each side of the ship—would be packed tight, like books on a shelf. Cramped and in irons, chained in pairs by hands and feet, they would be unable to move at all or to turn or change position without hurting one another. When the ship heeled it was even worse. The heat and the stench became suffocating, and the sloshing of the latrine tubs, foul. When the weather was bad, John might keep the slaves for days on end below deck without coming up for fresh air. But in doing so, disease and utter despair would settle like a dark cloud. John knew from other captains that sometimes half the slaves would die before some ships reached the West Indies.

Eight-and-a-half months after they arrived on the Guinea coast, when they had reached 80 percent of their capacity, the *African* sailed for the island of St. Kitts in the Caribbean. John hoped that the lighter cargo would yield a better return, but the results were mixed.

As they neared St. Kitts, John ordered all the slaves have their heads shaved in order to brighten their appearance. He was able to sell all the slaves quickly, and just like he had done with the *Duke of Argyle*, John made careful entries in his log at the conclusion of the trade.

"Two hundred seven slaves purchased.

Forty dead on the Middle Passage.

One hundred sixty-seven sold."

John knew they were not great numbers. The death rate was higher than on the *Argyle*, though at least the crew fared better, with only one fatality among them.

That, at least, was something to thank God for.

Having spent eight months at home with Polly after his first voyage, John only remained in England for eight weeks after his second. Despite high deaths and low profits, Manesty offered him a third journey as captain due to set sail in October 1753. John did not hesitate to take command of the *African* again.

The third voyage was always going to be different. He was older now, twenty-eight years of age, and far wiser thanks to his previous journeys. His heady optimism on the *Duke of Argyle* had been tempered by experience. John was now realistic about the slave trade, aware that there would be limited opportunities to trade on the Guinea coast. Finding good stock at reasonable prices would be even harder than it had been on previous journeys. He still wanted to do well by Manesty, too, of course, but sticking to a rigid target of 250 slaves was unwise. It was practically impossible to acquire them quickly enough to escape the many dangers that lay in wait.

John was wiser about the crew too. He was used to a high turnover of men between voyages and under no illusions that the majority of the new crewmen he welcomed aboard the *African* would be less wretched and vice-ridden than the last. Some would be loyal and trustworthy, while others would surely want to desert, spark a mutiny, or perhaps even kill their captain. He would have to watch them all carefully. And when the dangers revealed themselves, he would need to act.

Despite his seasoned outlook, John was looking forward to the voyage in some ways. For one, he was now convinced that the real benefit of being a Guinea trader was not so much the potential fortune he could make but the opportunity to spend a year or more with the shipboard solitude to read, write, and pray, attending to his own spiritual growth. With few distractions and plenty of time alone in his cabin, John was convinced that his time as a captain in the slave trade was a God-given gift that would allow him to mature as a Christian.

He was also excited about the fact that he had secured a post on board for an old friend from HMS *Harwich*, Job Lewis. Job was a good man who was going through hard times, and John was happy to help him out. The way John saw it, Job would benefit from both the employment and the opportunity to go deeper in his own spiritual journey. They could rise early together, walk the decks as they talked and prayed, study two or three chapters of the Bible in John's cabin, all before breakfast, then lead the rest of the crew in a devotional service and Scripture lesson on Sundays. They would be like two pilgrims journeying together in pursuit of a closer walk with God.

The *African* arrived on the Guinea coast without incident. However, soon John's leadership skills were tested. The ship's carpenter got a little riled one day when John was off the ship. He refused an officer's orders and caused serious offense to the second mate, and John had to make a difficult decision.

Should he punish him appropriately and put the man in irons and chain him on deck for days on end, or—since the barricado was not yet finished—should he show a little leniency and get the man back to work quickly? John chose the latter, and two days after receiving two dozen lashes, the carpenter was back at work.

There was another incident when a crewman deserted while on the coast, but it was of little consequence to John. He remained focused on his own spiritual journey, digging deeper into prayer and study of the Bible every day, even though Job Lewis's attendance was poor.

What did rattle John's peaceful routine were the reports from other trading ships that were circulating. The *Adventure* had been taken over by an insurrection, the *Racehorse* stolen by some local traders, while another trader had seen three of its crew killed in Kittam. Every experienced trader was used to the inevitable lean times that came, but now trade was so slow, and traders were unwilling to negotiate, so business was looking far worse than it ever had.

Between the challenges of supply, the oppressive humidity, and the noise, heat, and smoke that greeted him whenever he arrived at a factory, town, or trading post, John was running out of patience. Business was not the thrill it had once been, and he was forced to accept an awkward truth: the slave trade was not going to make him rich.

Perhaps we may not be rich—no matter, he wrote to Polly. *We are rich in Love.*

In addition to reassessing the true prospects of trade, John was also forced to reconsider his position on his friend Job. He had not embraced the spiritual pilgrimage that John had offered. In fact, he had become something of a bad influence on the rest of the crew. His long and loud outbursts laced with profanities entertained the crew, but they left John feeling distinctly upset.

John was realistic, but he was not a fool. The theft of the *Racehorse* presented him with an opportunity. It was half the size of the *African* but well-made with copper sheeting on the hull. When a Susu trader offered to sell it for a reasonable price of £130, John agreed. He transferred a small crew from the *African* and gave command of the vessel to Job, instructing him to remain on the coast and continue trading while the *African* took her eighty-seven slaves directly to St. Kitts. It was a good plan that would allow John to escape the Guinea coast after just four months of trading.

The *African* waited on the coast while the *Racehorse* was fitted out and readied for trade, during which time Job Lewis died. John saw no reason to change his plans and appointed another captain in his place.

Leaving Africa with a skeleton crew and under ninety slaves in the hold, John felt as though he had been released from Evans's chains all over again. He had never known so much turmoil, so much fighting, and so much death upon the coast. The trade had changed, and he was grateful to have escaped with all of his crew—not counting Job Lewis—and all of his slaves. For once, nobody had died. This was unheard of. I have *buried neither White, nor Black,* he wrote to Mary. *Let us praise God for his singular goodness to us.*

Not long into the Middle Passage, several of the crew fell ill. John distributed much of his food and drink among them and hoped their recovery would be swift. Then he started to feel unwell himself. His eyes became sore and his limbs ached beyond that which was in any way usual for him. He was robbed of all his energy; he could feel his temperature rise by the hour. Soon he was gripped by a fever more violent than either of those he had experienced on Plantain Island. He was weak and delirious, pain raking at his eyes and head, unable to leave his sweat-soaked sheets on his cabin bed. Hours crept by, each second more agonizing than the last. When sleep finally came, his dreams were lucid and terrifying. When he woke, he wondered if there was any surviving a fever as bad as this. He had seen many others suffer like this. None of them had lived.

He became terrified by the thought that he might die in the middle of the Atlantic Ocean. To perish thousands of miles away from his bride, thousands of miles away from every friend he had in the world, was truly horrifying to him. Would he be condemned to spend eternity as a lost and wandering soul?

Struggling against the pain, he did what he knew he must: he prepared himself for eternity.

First, he prayed. Short, breathless prayers that sounded more like whispers as he begged for God's mercy.

Then, his hand barely able to hold the pen, his eyes unable to focus on the page, he wrote to his wife. John was ready to die if this was his time, but he wanted nothing more than that Mary would be ready too.

> *I have been ill three days of a fever, which, though it is at present attended with no symptoms, particularly dangerous, it behoves me to consider, may terminate in death. I have endeavoured to compose myself to the summons, if it should so prove. . . . If I go now, in a few years, perhaps much sooner, you will follow me, I hope, in the same path, depending wholly on the divine mercy, through faith in the blood and mediation, of Jesus Christ our Redeemer.*

The fever gripped him for more than a week before it broke. Recovery was not swift, especially with barely any provisions left to feed himself. For more than a month he lay, desperately weak and faint. The *African* finally dropped anchor by Sandy Point at St. Kitts. The slaves were sold, but John was still weak and barely able go about his business.

Having once more reckoned with his own frailty, John was encouraged by the discovery of a spiritual confidant in Alexander Clunie, a fellow ship's captain. Clunie was not carrying slaves but gunpowder, bound for Brimstone Hill Fortress to protect the island against the French. Clunie's home was around the corner from where Newton grew up in Wapping, but more importantly, he was a devout Christian to whom John could open his heart without reserve.

For nearly a month the two captains spent every evening together, sometimes talking about spiritual things until the sun came up. It was another religious awakening for John. He had so much still to learn about God and his grace. He wrote in his diary, "I see that I had not that perfect dependence on Jesus my Saviour and him only for justification and acceptance." And as he prepared to sail for Liverpool, he added, "O Lord . . . may his example stir me up to go and do likewise, to endeavour to teach others those comforts wherewith I myself have been comforted."

Months later, Mary Newton stands quietly on Lord Street in Liverpool, watching the small crowd that has gathered outside St. Peter's Church. John is at the center of it all, pinning up a handwritten notice that details the success of his latest voyage. She feels the tears break free and run down her cheeks. She carefully removes from her sleeve the delicate cotton handkerchief—the very one that John brought back with him after his first command—folds it until it is small enough to fit in her hands, and discretely dries her face. Nobody sees her. They never do. They are all too busy watching her husband.

"Is it true?" a voice calls out.

"Every word," John says. "Your prayers and your blessings were instrumental in the success of the latest voyage of the *African*. Your petitions helped an African voyage perform without any disaster at all. Over these last several months we enjoyed something that I believe no other voyage of its kind has ever enjoyed. I serve notice that not one soul died throughout the entirety of the journey. Not one crewman. No, and not one slave either. All survived, thanks be to God."

The crowd murmur their approval, just as they have all over the city. Over the last several weeks, almost as soon as John returned from his second voyage on the *African*, he has visited plenty of churches like this. In a city where almost every person is somehow connected to the docks and the trade that flows in and out of them, John's story is the talk of the town. Everybody is talking about the vessel that returned from so dangerous a voyage without a single casualty.

Mary's tears are not tears of relief, however. They are not tears of gratitude either, though she is grateful beyond words that there were no deaths on board.

Mary's tears are not for her. They are for John.

She cries because in twelve days, he will be gone again, back on another voyage. Death, she fears, will have its appetite back. To complete one voyage without losing a soul is remarkable. To repeat it would be unthinkable.

She cries because even though her husband can stand and smile and shake the hands of well-wishers, she knows that so much of his story is left untold.

She alone knows the excruciating pain that afflicts his limbs whenever the weather turns cold. She alone is witness to the nightmares that plague him.

She alone hears him shout in the darkness about people called "Evans" and "Pee Eye" and "Jackson"—villains who lie in the shadows at night, waiting to devour him.

She alone knows the heavy, heavy price that being a captain demands of him.

Most of all, she cries because of how he looks as he stands outside these churches. For the first time in all the twelve years that she has known him, he looks and sounds completely at peace.

John makes his excuses and walks over to join Mary. The crowd follows, someone begs her pardon and squeezes past her to get closer to John. She moves a little to the side and waits for the moment to pass.

Being overlooked is nothing new to her. All her life people have shown more interest in her siblings than they have in her. Everyone in her family laughs louder, dances better, and is more comfortable in the focus of people's attention than she is. She knows that to most people her character is as unexciting as her looks are plain.

But John is not like most people. From the very first day they met—when her mother opened the front door, let out a cry of delight, and swept him inside the house—he had noticed her. Her siblings were dancing and chattering and all performing for his attention, yet as long as she was in the room, his eyes never strayed from her for more than a second.

Twelve years later, now man and wife, nothing has really changed. He seems more devoted than ever.

"My dear fellow," he calls to the man who moved her aside, his strong arm reaching out for her and pulling her close. "I have been separated long enough from my darling bride. I beg you do not keep us apart a moment longer!"

He is smiling, and there is laughter in the knot of people that surround them. Nobody speaks to their wife in public like John speaks to her. She feels people's eyes fall on her. There is a little envy from some, confusion from others. She blushes again and he takes her arm.

"Come, my dearest dear," he says softly before leading her away from the church. She glances up at his face. He has the same smile that he wore the day they were married.

These early winter days in Liverpool before he is to set sail again are precious. Each one is a gift more valuable than the day before. Still, the time is not all theirs. There is business to attend to, even more than usual given that his next command will be of the *Bee*, another new ship on her maiden voyage.

Neither of them want to be apart any longer than they have to, so Mary accompanies her husband wherever he goes. They flit between the docks and the offices of Joseph Manesty, checking inventory and scouring maps, selecting crewmen and inspecting the *Bee*. Mary does not know what she is looking at, cannot tell a *snow* from a *brig*, but she can read her husband as well as he can read a map. She can see the change that comes across him the moment he becomes Captain John Newton. His eyes lose their brightness. His voice grows weary. His hand does not reach for hers. Instead, he balls his hands into fists and holds them tight at his sides. Nobody else pays his hands any attention, but she does.

One afternoon, when his departure is so close that there are no more Sundays on which to visit churches, and his fists are almost permanently clenched at his sides, they take a walk to their favorite park—the one farthest away from the docks. They walk past the flowers in the pleasure gardens and head away from the music that beckons onlookers to the bandstand where two fiddlers are striking up a tune. They are drawn to the places where others are not, to find a bench where they can sit in peace.

The silence hangs lightly on them both.

"You are quite well?" she asks.

He nods.

"This slight breeze does not trouble you?"

A shake of the head.

The sound of the music in the distance fades in and out on the wind.

A minute later he turns to her and smiles.

"Forgive me," he sighs. "I am not good company today. You deserve better."

She takes his hand in hers. The silence is easy.

"Over these last six years"—he says as though carrying on a conversation they had only just paused—"so much has happened, and I have learned so much. I have read the Bible over and over. I have studied so many good books. And the Lord himself has taught me something of the evil of my heart. But those lessons have been hard-earned. For so long I traveled alone. On the *Greyhound*, on the *Duke of Argyle*, and on the *African* I had no one to whom I could turn. I struggled alone."

He pauses a while. His head drops. Mary waits.

"It was only on this last voyage, just as I recovered from the fever that afflicted me throughout the Middle Passage, that I finally met a man whose conversation was helpful to me. He not only informed my understanding, but his discourse inflamed my heart. He encouraged me to open my mouth in social prayer; he taught me the advantage of Christian converse; he put me upon an attempt to make my profession more public, and to venture to speak for God."

"You speak well. You are a bolder Christian than I ever could be," she says. "When you stand up in church it is as if all eyes and hearts are open to you. If people did not already know you to be a captain, I should think many would mistake you for a preacher." Mary pauses and wonders whether she should ask whether he would like to be a preacher. She thinks better of it.

John turns to her. "Polly, for so long I have been troubled by a great fear—the fear of relapsing into my former apostasy. But now I understand the covenant of grace. I expect to be preserved, but not by my own power and holiness. I am saved by the mighty power and promise of God, through faith in an unchangeable Savior. Knowing this truth, holding it here," he says, his fist on his chest, "my sun is seldom clouded."

Another strain of music washes over them. She recognizes the tune—a sea shanty that she has heard men singing on the docks. Mary feels the first chill of evening as the sun begins to set. "I shall pray for you, John. Every day while you are on the *Bee*, not an hour shall go by when I will not remember you and ask for God's protection upon you."

She shifts on the bench, ready to return to the rooms that Manesty has rented for them, but John is oblivious to her. He isn't moving. He is staring at the ground.

"I . . ." he starts, struggling to find the next words. "Since I recovered from my fever, I have been praying but one prayer. That the Lord, in his own time, would be pleased to fix in me a more humane calling."

Mary waits for John to say more, but no words come.

"My dear, I do not understand. A 'more humane calling'?"

"The slave trade," he says, as if the words themselves are so heavy that just saying them leaves him weak. "When I am going about the business of the trade, I am nothing but a gaoler. A turnkey. All my days are full of chains and shackles and bolts. To spend one's days in such employment, it is . . . shocking."

He looks at her. "And these long separations. They are hard to bear. I hope that the Lord will make me free of them one day."

Two days before the departure of the *Bee*, Mary accompanies John on his final visit to Manesty's offices. There are more maps and papers and conversations about which carpenter would be best suited for the voyage.

Mary watches her husband closely. The nightmares have been worse these last few nights, so bad he has barely slept at all. It is dark in Manesty's office, and the lack of light makes him look even paler than he was in the park. She checks his hands. They are thrust deep into the pockets of his heavy, woolen sea jacket. She can see the fabric strain where his fists are.

"Yes," Manesty is saying from behind his desk, "you were wise to leave the Guinea coast so early on the *African*. You should do the same again on the *Bee*. Trade fast and sail faster, eh? But perhaps a few more than eighty-seven this time? Even if you have to buy a bunch of rebels like before, just double-chain them the whole way. I've made sure you have plenty of collars on board this time."

Manesty carries on for a few more minutes, prattling on about the rise in prices and the challenges of making a profit, but Mary is no longer listening. She is staring at John, who is staring back at his employer, giving an impression of listening to everything he is saying, but his eyes are glazed. Mary watches beads of sweat start to form on his brow.

When Manesty is finished, Mary hurries John back to their lodgings. She orders tea from the landlady and urges John to rest in a chair. Before he can sit, he slumps forward and onto the dark-red rug under their feet.

Mary screams.

John lies on his side, arms and legs twisted and twitching uncontrollably. Mary calls for help, then falls to her knees and tries to comfort her husband.

"My darling!" she calls. "John!"

It is no use. He cannot hear her, no matter what she says. No touch soothes him. Nothing calms him. All she can do is watch as he lies thrashing on the carpet. His face is contorted, eyes rolling, spittle forming at the corners of his mouth.

Nothing like this has ever happened before. There has been no hint that John was unwell. Mary is sobbing uncontrollably. The landlady has arrived and is shouting again for the doctor, her voice so loud Mary thinks it might bring down the ceiling.

And then, just as soon as it started, John's seizure ends.

"John," she soothes, her hand on his brow. He is burning so hot it frightens her to touch him. "John, my darling. I am here. All is well."

She strokes his hair and takes the cold, wet handkerchief that the landlady hands her and presses it on his forehead.

"Shh," she soothes, as if he were a child. "It is over now. You are safe."

John's breathing is shallow, his eyes locked shut.

"John!" she calls, risking a gentle shake on the shoulder. "John. Wake up."

She shouts, then whispers. Shakes, then caresses him. She places her head on his chest and prays. No matter what she tries, nothing works. John is locked away from her. She cannot wake him.

For a whole hour she stays there, kneeling on the floor next to her husband. Tears come and go, but all the time the panic rises in her throat, flooding her from within.

And then, without warning, he opens his eyes.

She hugs him tight. Tighter than ever before. So tight she thinks she will never let him go again.

Part 2

And grace will lead me home.

The church of St. Peter and St. Paul in the village of Olney was full, just as it always was these days. The pews were packed tight, the air thick with the murmur of hundreds of excited voices. It was standing-room only in the gallery above—the same gallery that had been installed months earlier to try to cope with the increased attendance since John's first sermon at the church.

John sat at the front, Mary at his side, and he closed his eyes. More than a decade had passed since he captained the *African*, and he had not sailed since. But something about the noise of the crowd at his back reminded him of his days on board—especially the times when the crew grew restless and rowdy. He felt the same nervous feeling then that he felt now, knowing that if he failed to secure their attention and direct their thoughts, chaos would ensue.

"You are sure this is wise?" Mary asked.

It was a reasonable question, but not one that he intended spending a good deal of time considering. He squeezed her hand as he stood up, then leaned close and whispered, "Never deliberate."

John took his place at the front of the church, looked out at the mass of faces, and ignored a slight tremor of nerves. With more than two hundred children gathered for the Thursday morning meeting, and not even a handful of adults on hand to supervise them, the challenge was great. He had to win them over, just like a captain with a crew who had too much time on their hands.

He stood and waited. Silence was typically slow to arrive on these children's church meetings. But it would come. It always did.

He waited some more.

"I wonder," he said as the last of the talkers clammed up. "I wonder whether there be a boy or a girl here today who would like to see a dead body."

At first there was more silence. Four hundred eyes locked on him, some wide with wonder, some narrowed in disbelief.

"It really is dead," John added. "Dead and waiting to be buried."

Then came the raised arms. In ones and twos at first, isolated clusters of children scattered around the church nave. Before long John was looking at a whole forest of waving hands as the church started to hum once again with the sound of excited children.

"Very well," he said, his hands held out for quiet. "I shall show every one of you that wishes to see. We have a body laid out at the front of the church for burial. But whether you choose to look upon the body or not, think on this: The man died in the firm assurance that he would be welcomed into heaven. He lived well. He was a good man. He did not curse or blaspheme or break the Lord's commandments. But none of these are the reason for his confidence in his salvation. He did not die in peace because of the good things he believed he had done. He died in peace because he knew that all the wrong things he had done had been forgiven by Jesus himself. Only by acknowledging his sin could he receive God's mercy. Grace is the greatest gift that has ever been given. We can only find it on our knees."

The church was silent. John caught Mary's eye. She smiled at him and nodded.

"Never deliberate," she mouthed.

John's journey to the church at Olney, Buckinghamshire, had started the moment he lay unconscious on the floor of his Liverpool lodgings. During the hour that he was unresponsive, his whole world was changing. By the time he stumbled to his feet, his fate had been decided. Manesty could never risk placing the command of the *Bee,* or any of his ships, in the hands of a man who might pass out at any moment. This the doctors had confirmed. Though his seizure was inexplicable, his career as a Guinea trader, or sailor of any kind, was over.

John's unspoken prayer had been answered.

The new desire to serve the church was as strong as the previous calling of the sea. Just like his path to becoming a captain, there were storms and setbacks on his route to ordination, hard lessons to be learned and good people who helped guide his steps. None of it happened quickly, however. The dawning of the light was slow. It took longer than he hoped, but he made nothing like the same number—or manner—of mistakes he made as a young man. With the encouragement of his wife and the conviction that his life had been spared for a reason, he persisted, laying the foundations for a life of service in the church that was as solid and sure as the timbers in a hundred-ton hull.

For ten years he worked on land at the port of Liverpool, studied hard, told his story of a sinner saved by mercy to all who would listen. He threw himself into ministry near and far. He could feel the spiritual awakening that was spreading across the land, like the tide coming in, and he wanted to be a part of it. People were waking up to the need for a more personal faith in Christ— something much more than conventional religion. Traveling lay preachers, earnest small groups for fellowship, fervent hymn singing, heartfelt testimonies of conversion, impassioned praying, people poring over the Bible like it was written just for them—the signs were everywhere. He had missed all this while he was at sea. But he could see clearly now the path before him. He would help others find the living faith that had found him.

Eventually, after years of preparing and knocking on closed doors, John was ordained in the Church of England and given a parish less than a day's ride north of London. The pulpit, rather than the quarterdeck, would be his new home. A town of two thousand souls awaited his arrival, and it was through the storms of life he would guide his new crew to safe harbor.

He could speak about the love of God with conviction, knowing that if he could be forgiven, then so could the most sin-sick soul in his parish.

About a year into his ministry, as he was getting to know his people, he rose to preach once more. He looked out over the congregation from the pulpit and down at the notes he had made for his sermon. He longed for hard hearts to be melted, just like his had been transformed in the midst of that North Atlantic storm. It was the mercy and love of God that could make all the difference:

Now are there any hearts so hard, so much like stones, so much like tigers, as to pay no regard to this love? It has been found that sinners who have

143

stood it out against the terrors and judgments of God and denounced in his word have been captivated and melted down by love. Are there any here that have added sin to sin, through despair of mercy, thinking all help was past—O say not so, see how God has loved the world—there is indeed then forgiveness with him. . . . Let us chide our cold unfeeling hearts—and pray for a coal of fire from the heavenly altar to send us home in a flame of love to him who has thus loved us.

As a clergyman, the Reverend John Newton relished the unconventional, but never for the sake of it. He preferred his blue woolen sea coat to new clerical robes because his old coat was warmer, even if it was getting just a little snug around the belly. He published his bestselling autobiography—*An Authentic Narrative of Some Remarkable and Interesting Particulars in the Life of **********—not because he was hungry for fame in his early forties but because of his appetite for sharing the truth. His life was a monument to God's great mercy. You don't celebrate a monument: you celebrate what it points to.

He brought singing masters to teach the children to sing, not to entertain or distract but to connect. He visited the sick outside his parish boundaries because their own vicar was too lazy to do so. He preached for one hour, with just a few notes, because he had a saving message to proclaim. He issued tickets for the Tuesday evening prayer meetings because he wanted to know that those who attended were truly serious about their faith. He visited the lacemakers—of which there were more than twelve hundred in the parish—at their cottages, hunched over their bobbins and pillows and lacework, because they were too poor to take a break and visit him. He wrote his own hymns and set them to familiar tunes because the regular folk in the pews found the metrical psalms with their dull tunes hard to understand and even harder to sing. He preached frequently, often six times a week, because there were always more people clamoring to hear the good news. He gave a "funeral turn" to his preaching when there were dead bodies laid out in church, not to fill people with fear of death but to flood them with hope of life everlasting beyond the grave.

His days fell into a steady rhythm. Most mornings he would spend reading and writing, feeding on Scripture, turning to the Lord in prayer. He would kneel to pray for his friends, then move to his desk and write to them words of encouragement, guidance, and insight.

I have been thinking of you and yours upon my knees, he wrote to one friend who had been struggling greatly. It was a greeting that he could have written many times over.

Afternoons he reserved for his parishioners. He was determined to devote himself to their care and would spend an hour at a time meeting them individually. He recorded the names of those he visited, some who traveled great distances to sit with him in his study, others he met with in their own homes. As he wrote to Mary, not long after arriving in Olney, *An old woman came after me, and invited me to her cottage. I went. Five or six women soon joined us. We talked, sung a hymn, and I prayed.* Soon he had regular prayer meetings in cottages, barns, and villages all around Olney. At times he would take parishioners with him on his rounds or encourage spiritually mature lay people to visit the ill and afflicted.

The people he served needed him. There were heartbreaking cases of mental illness, suicides and attempted suicides, poverty, and alcoholism. He breakfasted with a father who was distressed by the unhappy conduct and elopement of his daughter; he called day after day on a dying man at nearby Weston Underwood to establish him in the hope of eternal life; and he spent time with a couple at Warrington, seeking to comfort them after their thirteen-year-old son was killed in an overturned cart.

He needed to care for the bodies and souls of all. He even used one of the new "electrical machines" that medical people were employing to try to help the sick. He treated a woman with rheumatic disorder who was soon after converted under his preaching. In an age where some religious elites felt little need to make themselves or the gospel available to their flock, the pastor John Newton was happily taking a different path. He was building a nurturing spiritual community, and the results were clear for all to see.

The genuine spiritual awakening he had seen in London, in the northwest, and elsewhere had definitely come to Olney and it was rapidly spreading beyond the town. It was all John could do to keep up. Men and women were hungry for the message of salvation.

So when he first met the newly widowed Mary Unwin, her children, and her close friend, Mr. William Cowper—a name that rhymes with *shooter* not *shouter*—John did what instinct insisted he do: he invited them all to move to Olney and stay with him and Mary in the vicarage. They could share in what God was doing in the town.

John knew little about William Cowper at first. He knew he was a well-educated man of letters. He knew that he had experienced much more than his share of grief and sorrow in life. Most of all, though, he knew that William was a man in need of a friend.

William Cowper's long acquaintance with suffering started at birth. Not his, but the birth of his younger brother. William was two days away from his sixth birthday when baby John was born and his mother died. Even late in life he remembered poignantly his feelings of loss at the time: "My mother! when I learn'd that thou wast dead, / Say, wast thou conscious of the tears I shed?"

There were other siblings as well—five of them—yet none survived childhood except his brother John. The suicide of a family friend planted a poisoned seed within young William's mind. The seed grew when he was sent away to boarding school aged nine, where he was bullied by older pupils. It grew within him like a twisted briar, and by the time he was an adult, William suffered from a depression that was almost suffocating. He could be convivial in company but he was often dying on the inside. He was prone to withdraw into his own thoughts with too little armor to protect him from irrational fears and punishing self-doubt.

Yet he was gifted, especially with words. His mind was sharp and words bent to his will like timber in the hands of a skilled woodworker. Even more, he had a feeling for beauty that was unmistakable when he wrote. He relished serious study, especially the classics, and found himself on the path to becoming a lawyer—a path set out for him by his highly respected father. Though intellectually capable, William felt unsuited to a profession that relied so heavily on public performance, and the burden soon became crippling. "Day and night," he wrote of an anxiety attack that lasted a full year, "I was upon the rack, lying down in horrors and despair."

Prayer helped, as did spending time in nature. Later, in one of his most famous poems, he would write: "God made the country, and man made the town." But relief was only ever temporary. At times he wondered whether the few moments of heaven-sent peace he had experienced were merely an illusion.

Worrying about money and quietly in love with his cousin, one day he found himself hoping that the clerk of the journals in the House of Lords—a senior legal post—would die so that he might be nominated for the post by his well-connected uncle. It was a foolish thought and he felt bad for dwelling on it. He felt even worse when the man really did die and he was offered the position.

The prospect of taking on the job was terrifying to him, especially when it was contested and he would have to appear before the bar of the House and defend himself in a public inquisition. He was trapped. The closer he got to the public hearing, the more he panicked. He sensed that a mighty storm was coming or that death itself might be imminent. Something was happening to him. He railed against God, believing that there was no point in asking for help or mercy, for God would surely never give it. He saw himself as a spiritual outsider, an outcast whose only escape would come when he finally gave in to the insanity that seemed to be crouching in the shadows. He was spiraling out of control.

He attempted to kill himself instead. First it was poison. Then he tried throwing himself in the Thames. Finally, he stabbed himself with his pen-knife, strung a noose from his chamber door, and hung himself on it long enough to lose consciousness and fall to the floor. When he came to, he sent for his uncle and told him of his troubles. His uncle intervened so that the post at the House of Lords was no longer his to worry about, but any relief that the crisis was over was short-lived. Because now, in place of anxiety came guilt. Surely God would punish him for trying to end his life. What else could he expect besides death and eternal punishment? He saw demons prowling in the shadows as he gave himself up to utter despair. He had lost everything. His first words to his brother were, "Oh brother, I am damned." He soon became incoherent altogether.

His brother arranged for him to be admitted to an asylum in the country-side north of London, where he spent eight long months tortured by his religious delusions. He was convinced that he was "devoted to destruction" by an angry God. At last, however, the first signs of a breakthrough emerged when he read about Lazarus. He started to wonder about the depths of love and mercy on display when Jesus raised his friend from the dead. Two months later, he woke one morning, completely free from despair, with the sure knowledge that the same mercy that was offered to Lazarus was being extended to him.

It opened the door to hope and opened his eyes to what he read in his Bible. Reading Romans 3:25 about Christ's death and "remission of sins that are past," he was struck by the truth. "Immediately the full beams of the sun of righteousness shone upon me. I saw the sufficiency of the atonement He had made, my pardon sealed in His blood, and all the fullness and completeness of my justification. In a moment I believed and received the Gospel."

He left the asylum feeling stronger than he had at any other point in his life. He chose not to return to London but to stay with friends, Morley and Mary Unwin. The family embraced him, inviting him to live with them and share their simple lives. Mary Unwin seemed like the mother he had lost all those years ago. They talked about faith and enjoyed the seclusion and solitude of the countryside. Everyone was reading Newton's *An Authentic Narrative*, and they all hoped that one day they would meet the author. Life was good. There were still long intervals of darkness that troubled William, but at last they were interrupted by regular bursts of joy.

William Cowper did get to meet the author of *An Authentic Narrative*. It happened as life was once again overshadowed by grief when Morley Unwin died suddenly after he was thrown from his horse. As William tried to comfort Mary and her two children, they received a visit. It was John and Mary Newton. A friend had suggested the Newtons visit, but they arrived to find it a house of mourning.

By the time the Newtons left that day, one thing was sure: William and John were set to become fast friends.

John pushed his chair away from his desk, took the piece of paper that William was handing him, and started to read. Intuition told him that William would far rather John read it silently. John looked up, then looked back at the page and started to read out loud.

"Struck by that light . . ."

William let out a low groan of protest. John shot his friend a mock frown, cleared his throat, and started again.

Struck by that light, the human heart,
A barren soil no more,
Sends the sweet smell of grace abroad,
Where serpents lurk'd before.

John paused, his eyes taking in the words a second time, then a third. He noticed William wince a little. This was obviously still too personal. William had written these lines not long after his conversion, while still at the asylum.

John handed back the page and took a long look at his friend. "Perfect," he said. "It is perfect. You have written something far better than I could have ever hoped for."

John was both amazed and impressed. A few days earlier he had mentioned to his friend that he was intending to preach on Isaiah 35. His suggestion that William try writing a hymn to accompany it was more for William's benefit than for the congregation's. Yet what William had written was so far beyond his expectations.

"I was hoping it might serve for the sermon," added William, "since I was reflecting in these lines on the promise in verse seven that 'parched ground shall become a pool, and the thirsty land springs of water.' This has been my experience."

From his earliest childhood memories, John knew the power of hymns, and as a preacher he knew the limits of his sermons. He wanted people to be able to experience the grace and mercy of God for themselves, to open themselves up to a knowledge that went beyond the head and straight to the heart. Verses like William's, set to stirring music, had real power. Almost immediately John could see that this was a wonderful opportunity to strengthen the faith of those in his care.

There was another benefit on offer. Ever since William, Mary Unwin, and her two children had moved to Olney—first living with John and Mary in the vicarage for almost half a year, then taking the house directly across the meadow behind—John and William had been inseparable. Most mornings William would accompany John on his pastoral visits, but not as a silent partner or mute observer. William would happily sit and talk with lacemakers while they worked at their pillows. He would listen to the sick and the dying and pray with them as they unburdened themselves before death. They felt like they knew him and said he was a comfort in their distress. He seemed to understand. He was even able to laugh through the chaos and noise of the Thursday morning meetings attended by more than two hundred local children. He reached out like a lay pastor to the whole parish.

But there were also those moments when William appeared incapable of offering help to others. The clouds would roll over unannounced, the smile would vanish from his lips. William would fade from his surroundings and John would know that he was once more in the valley of the shadow of death. John could recognize a bruised and battered ship when he saw one.

John hoped that by encouraging William to join him in writing hymns to accompany his weekly sermons, he might keep him from the lowest reaches of the valley floor. And it was an opportunity for him to make a difference. After all, he knew this was what William wanted. "My sole drift is to be useful," William would say.

At first, it appeared to work. John and William shared hymn-writing duties, though it was perfectly clear which one of them had the real talent with the pen. John felt his own verses were often forced and clumsy, lacking in both poetry and flair. But William was able to write verses that shone bright with life and hope and truth, even if he had simply been commissioned to mark the opening of a new room for their prayer meeting. There was a quiet trust and repose in the prayer:

> *Jesus, where'er thy people meet,*
> *There they behold thy mercy-seat;*
> *Where'er they seek thee, thou art found,*
> *And ev'ry place is hallow'd ground.*

Though he had written some hymns before, in 1772 William took up this task with renewed vigor. Before long he was even borrowing John's favorite sea metaphors and using them to add creative power:

> *O Lord, the pilot's part perform,*
> *And guide and guard me thro' the storm. . . .*

> *Tho' tempest-toss'd and half a wreck,*
> *My Saviour thro' the floods I seek;*
> *Let neither winds nor stormy main,*
> *Force back my shatter'd bark again.*

William wrote with craft and skill, but always from the heart. He knew the human condition. He knew what it felt like when faith was strong:

> *There is a fountain fill'd with blood*
>   *Drawn from Emmanuel's veins;*
> *And sinners, plung'd beneath that flood,*
>   *Lose all their guilty stains. . . .*

> *E'er since, by faith, I saw the stream*
>   *Thy flowing wounds supply:*
> *Redeeming love has been my theme,*
>   *And shall be till I die.*

But he could also identify with the experience of alienation and desolation:

> *Where is the blessedness I knew*
>   *When first I saw the Lord?*
> *Where is the soul-refreshing view*
>   *Of Jesus, and his word?*

> *What peaceful hours I once enjoy'd!*
>   *How sweet their mem'ry still!*
> *But they have left an aching void,*
>   *The world can never fill.*

After sixty-seven hymns, though, William told John he felt he could write no more. The onset of a renewed depression was too fierce, too suffocating to try to create lyrics. He was back in the valley of the shadow of death. How could anyone hope to lift a congregation's spirit when he was so crushed by fear and despair?

Even though it was the middle of summer, the sun had not yet risen when Mary Unwin knocked at the door of the vicarage.

"Please," she begged from the garden below as John leaned out of his bedroom window. Even in the darkness he could see that she had dressed hurriedly, with a lace shawl wrapped around her shoulders. She opened her mouth to say more, but the words would not come. There was no need for her to say any more. John rushed out of the house and followed her home.

He found William awake in the parlor but vacantly gazing into the fire, all color drained from his face.

"William?" John tried to rouse him, but he did not respond.

John leaned close and placed a hand upon his friend's arm. It was trembling. "William. My dear brother. May I sit with you awhile?"

They remained in almost perfect silence. The only sound in the room were the occasional staggered intakes of breath as William tried to force air into his lungs. The candle burned low. The sun rose.

William had relapsed into a deep melancholy, unable to shake its grip for several days. John wrote to Mary, "Dear Sir Cowper is in the depths as much as ever."

For the next six months John stayed even closer to William than usual, especially on those days when William's spirits sank again. There were occasional trips to the lacemakers, but no visits to the sick or the dying. John did not ask his friend to write any hymns, but they walked often, sometimes talking, sometimes not. They could spend hours together in nature, meandering along the winding River Ouse, watching the slow changes as summer faded, autumn settled, and the cold fingers of winter took hold.

John had always liked to mark significant dates, especially personal anniversaries—such as his first encounter with Polly or the storm on the *Greyhound*. As the year drew to a close and Christmas passed, his thoughts turned to his sermon on January 1, 1773. It was time for a fresh start for them all.

It was not difficult to find a theme for the sermon. Every new year he paused to take stock, to look back on how God had provided and led them faithfully, even through difficulties. And then he looked ahead. Aware of the sands of time, he felt conscious that every day was a gift. He wrote in his diary,

Friday the 1st January. This is the Ninth New Years day I have seen in this place. I have reason to say The Lord crowneth every year with his goodness. . . . I am now in the 49th year of my age, and may expect in the course of a few years at most to go whence I shall no more return, nor have I a certainty of continuing here a single year or even a month or a day. May thy grace keep me always waiting till my appointed change shall come.

He realized that grace had brought him safe thus far, and he trusted that grace would lead him home. As he considered that the biblical King David must have felt the same way when God announced his gracious promises to the Israelite ruler, despite his sinful past, the sermon took care of itself. The hymn, however, was a whole other challenge.

By the time John stood behind the lectern at St. Peter and St. Paul on the morning of Friday, January 1, 1773, and looked out at the congregation, he was ready.

His text for the sermon was just two verses long, 1 Chronicles 17:16–17. He savored every syllable as his rich, powerful voice flooded the church.

And David the king came and sat before the LORD, and said, Who am I, O LORD God, and what is mine house, that thou hast brought me hitherto? And yet this was a small thing in thine eyes, O God; for thou hast also spoken of thy servant's house for a great while to come, and hast regarded me according to the estate of a man of high degree, O LORD God.

He paused, eyed his notes once more, then looked up and paused again to look into the faces of these people he loved so dearly. It was an important moment. There, too, was his friend William Cowper, who had been brought through many dangers, toils, and snares and yet still walked closely with God. It was a time for gratitude.

"The Lord bestows many blessings upon his people, but unless he likewise gives them a thankful heart, they lose much of the comfort they might have in them."

It was a simple sermon. Three sections each divided into three clear points. First, he urged people to join with David in the question, "Who am I?" Second, to always remember the wretched state God found us in. He encouraged them to recall the many dangers God brought them through, to see how mercy and grace have followed them always. Third, he spoke of the future: "He found us upon the dunghill and has made us companions of princes—in a wilderness and has led us to the City of God."

In closing, John delivered his strongest words: God's mercy and grace are real, but we must play our part to receive them.

"We are spared thus far. But some, I fear, are strangers to the promises. You are entered upon a New Year. It may be your last. You are at present barren trees in the vineyard. O fear lest the sentence should go forth. Cut it down."

The sermon over, John sat down. He had hoped to have been able to preach with freedom and passion, to inspire some great change in the lives of those barren trees in the congregation, but instead he felt a little flat. His heart felt strangely unaffected by it all.

On cue, the congregation stood to sing. John introduced the hymn by the name he had given it, *Faith's Review and Expectation*. Just as he looked backward and forward every New Year's Day, aware of God's grace in his life, and just as King David looked backward and forward in response to God's faithfulness, so John could present this as a model for his congregation. He hoped the simple song would do a better job than his sermon.

> *Amazing grace! (how sweet the sound)*
> *That saved a wretch like me!*
> *I once was lost, but now am found,*
> *Was blind, but now I see.*
>
> *'Twas grace that taught my heart to fear,*
> *And grace my fears reliev'd;*

How precious did that grace appear,
The hour I first believ'd!

Through many dangers, toils and snares,
I have already come;
'Tis grace has brought me safe thus far,
And grace will lead me home.

This was the key turning point in the hymn, and Newton hoped the congregation could also make the turn to face the future with faith. They sang the last three stanzas, tracing God's hand of grace through the balance of their lives, the certain encounter with death, and the end of all things:

The Lord has promis'd good to me,
His word my hope secures;
He will my shield and portion be,
As long as life endures.

Yes, when this flesh and heart shall fail
And mortal life shall cease;
I shall possess, within the veil,
A life of joy and peace.

The earth shall soon dissolve like snow,
The sun forbear to shine;
But GOD, who called me here below,
Will be forever mine.

John poured the tea and handed the cup over. He ignored the slight rattling of William's cup in the saucer.

"Are you cold?" John asked when William did away with the saucer and cradled the cup in his hands. "Should I add more wood to the fire?"

"No. I am quite well. Thank you."

"You are looking well."

William stared into his teacup. "Today is a good day."

"Indeed it is," said John. "I was pleased to see you in church this morning."

"I was pleased to be there. Especially to hear your new hymn." He put down his cup and looked his friend long in the eye. "''Twas grace that taught my heart to fear, and grace my fears relieved.' You have improved, my dear friend."

John returned the smile. "In you I have both a good tutor and an excellent muse."

The fire crackled. It was warm in John's study. William sat back and stared at the grate.

"I believe I may have another hymn for you soon," William said.

"You might? That is excellent news. Today's attempt was fair, but the others . . ."

William wasn't listening. He closed his eyes and exhaled slowly.

"God moves in a mysterious way," he began. "His wonders to perform. He plants his footsteps in the sea, and rides upon the storm."

John sat still and listened to the next stanzas, knowing better than to interrupt.

> *Ye fearful saints, fresh courage take,*
> *The clouds ye so much dread,*
> *Are big with mercy . . .*

William opened his eyes and looked at John. "I fear it is a little dark."

"No. It is true. I believe it with all my heart."

William brushed the compliment away. "Perhaps you are right. I know how hard it is to discern God's ways."

William continued,

> *Blind unbelief is sure to err,*
> *And scan his work in vain;*
> *God is his own interpreter,*
> *And He will make it plain.*

Later that day, John received a visit from William. He had been walking alone in the fields, then put the finishing touches on the hymn. He showed it to John that evening. Both agreed that it should be added to the book of hymns they were hoping to publish. It was a good day, and a great start to the new year.

Early on January 2, however, while the skies were dark and the daylight was hours away, Mary Unwin urgently sent a servant to fetch the Newtons. There was a loud, repeated knock on the door of the vicarage. There was no need to say anything. John and Mary rushed from the house to be by William's side.

This time the depression was even deeper, and a terrible religious dementia had overwhelmed him. He had harmed himself, tormented by the appalling lure of suicide and in imminent danger of killing himself. He was convinced that he was a Judas, a man singled out by God to be damned for all eternity. No matter what John or Mary said, no matter how they prayed, they could not convince him of the truth of God's grace, love, and mercy. All they could do was sit with him and trust that the darkness would eventually pass.

But the crisis deepened in the following days. In a terrifying dream in February, William heard words spoken over him with great finality: "It is all over with thee, thou hast perished." It was like God was telling William to kill himself.

John recorded his feelings, as ever, in his diary: "My dear friend still walks in darkness. I can hardly conceive that any one in a state of grace and favour with God can be in greater distress; and yet no one walked more closely with Him, or was more simply devoted to Him in all things."

William was held hostage by his fears and delusions. He thought everyone hated him. He worried that his food was poisoned. So John had William move in with him for fourteen months, and all of them—John, Mary, and Mary Unwin—were on continuous suicide watch, not letting him out of their sight for even a minute. John sought medical advice and arranged treatment. He even tried the electrical machine again. But all to no avail. A dark cloud had descended, and nothing seemed to make a difference.

Eventually, ever so slowly, John noticed that William had discovered ways to keep his mind occupied. He sketched, worked in the garden, kept rabbits, and wrote poetry about the tranquil landscapes around him. He resumed his classical studies. But his faith was burned out.

"You know the comfort I have had there," he would say, pointing at the church whenever John invited him to attend a service. "I have seen the glory of the Lord in his house, and until I can go there I'll not go anywhere else."

January 1, 1773—the day William sat with the rest of the parishioners in Olney and heard "Amazing Grace" sung for the first time—was the last day he ever attended church.

William's friendship with John would remain, though he would never fully recover. There would be other breakdowns to come, each one leaving deeper scars and frailer foundations. There would be no more hymns to write, but poetry would flow with the same raw honesty and poignancy that marked his hymns in Olney. He would become one of the century's greatest poets, especially celebrating the simple domestic scene where he lived, but he would lose all spiritual comfort. To John, this would be a sign of a man afflicted, not a sinner caught up in apostasy. He would write to William when they were separated,

> *Though your comforts have been so long suspended, I know not that I ever saw you for a single day since your calamity came upon you, in which I could not perceive as clear and satisfactory evidence, that the grace of God was with you, as I could in your brighter and happier times.*

Grace was always there, even in the darkest of places, even when he couldn't see or feel it.

Late in his life, William would write his final poem. Once again, he would borrow his old friend's favorite imagery of the sea, but it was a darkening sea that would fill his imagination. He would imagine a castaway lost at sea and compare this to his own condition:

We perish'd, each alone,
But I, beneath a rougher sea
And whelm'd in deeper gulphs than he.

He would turn to this same image in the last letter he ever wrote—to John. Looking back to the happier days they shared, he would lament, "I was little aware of what I had to expect, and that a storm was at hand which in one terrible moment would darken, and in another still more terrible, blot out that prospect for ever.—Adieu Dear Sir, whom in those days I call'd Dear friend."

Speaking at William's funeral in 1800, John would be equally honest about his friend.

"I don't know a person upon earth I consult upon a text of Scripture or any point of conscience so much to my satisfaction as Mr. Cowper. He could give comfort when he could not receive any himself."

For decades he tried to help William see the truth about God's love and mercy, desperate to find a way to help William's eyes open to God's grace, to show him the vast size and scale and power of God's love. He could not get through. William's eyes were too clouded by suffering, the light too weakened by sorrow.

And yet, throughout the years of their friendship, John gave his friend what he could. He stood with him. He held on tightly, held the faith for a suffering brother in Christ. A man who had lost the thread and who could not find his way.

To any casual observer, the heavy woolen sea coat and fondness for peppering his hymns and sermons with sailing metaphors were the clearest signs of John's past. Those who knew him a little better might understand why he looked a little less steady on his feet when the weather was cold or wet. It would take a fellow sailor to recognize the almost-faded calluses on his hands or—if they got that far—the faint scars on his back.

The real legacy of John's years as a sailor were not the outward signs and scars. Not at first, at least. The real legacy were the memories of horrors he had witnessed and the burden that he carried. This legacy did not rot like the timbers of a neglected vessel or fray like the threads of his coat. The memories of his former life were buried deep within him. Far away from prying eyes. Deep enough to almost be ignored. But John could not ignore what he had seen. Like seeds in the darkness, the memories grew.

After two centuries of British involvement in the slave trade—a period in which British ships like the *Duke of Argyle*, the *African*, and the *Bee* contributed to the transport of almost three million slaves across the Atlantic—public opinion was only just starting to change. There had been opponents of the trade over the years, but their voices had been few and easily ignored. Others, like the evangelist George Whitefield, had spoken out against the cruelty of slave owners in the American South, yet he eventually owned slaves of his own in Georgia. He was not alone, either. The Anglican Society for the Propagation of the Gospel in Foreign Parts branded their slaves across the chest with the word "Society." Throughout John Newton's time on board the Guinea ships, the slave trade was simply a fact of life for most Britons, as for most Europeans. There was an appalling but near universal blindness.

And yet change was coming.

It started with three Quakers in America. Benjamin Lay, John Woolman, and Anthony Benezet refused to accept that slave ownership was compatible with their faith. In 1754—the same year that John's seizure on the floor of the Liverpool boarding house brought an abrupt end to his own career as a slaver—the Philadelphia Quakers were the first Christian organization to denounce the practice of slaveholding.

Others joined them. In the decades that followed, Enlightenment philosophers and Christian activists and former slaves themselves gradually started to speak out, while missionaries traveled to the West Indies to work among the enslaved people there. Slowly, the tide was turning, and John found himself drawn ever closer into the orbit of the antislavery world.

It started after he staggered up from the carpet. It was the best part of a decade before he would reach Olney, but as well as working as a custom's officer in the port of Liverpool and trying to find a way to be ordained by the Anglican Church, John had started meeting people who were asking questions about the inhumanity of slavery and the slave trade. In 1755, Benjamin Fawcett, a Presbyterian minister, published a piece in which he wrote warmly and compassionately of African slaves as full brothers in Christ. Some years later, Fawcett and John struck up a friendship. Fawcett found John's stories of his previous life compelling enough that he asked him to write some of them down in a series of letters. He wanted to know in more detail how God had worked in his life through his experiences.

It was a simple enough request, but even though it was 1762 and John was two years away from being ordained and moving to Olney, he was in no mind to rush it. He wanted to wait until he could write freely. He wanted to write without interruption. He wanted to immerse himself in his memories and return without embellishments or exaggerations. He wanted to offer Fawcett the truth, nothing less.

His discovery was clear. "The most interesting parts of my story . . ." he wrote in an accompanying note to Fawcett, "happened many years ago, when I was neither capable of reflecting on them as I ought, nor desirous to retain them in my memory."

Across eight letters, John wrote honestly about his failings. He described himself on the *Harwich* as being driven by "hopeless desire, despair, and revenge." Of his time as the servant of slaves on Plantain Island, he wrote that he had "the prodigal's distress, but without the prodigal's reflection." He confessed to being a lout and a blasphemer, to seeing all his fine words and best Christian intentions turn to smoke. But when it came to the detail of his work as a slave trader, he was quiet. There was no mention of chains or thumbscrews or the air filling with screams as he divided a mother from her children in the pursuit of profit. It was too much. It was too soon.

This was the same year that Quaker Anthony Benezet published *A Short Account of That Part of Africa, Inhabited by the Negroes . . . and the Manner by Which the Slave-Trade Is Carried On*, in which he quoted a detailed account by a former slave trader who now sought "to atone for my Neglect of Duty as a Christian, in engaging in that wicked Traffic." The details sounded remarkably like Newton's experience on the *Brownlow*.

John wrote another longer series of letters to the Reverend Thomas Haweis, covering the same personal history he had written about previously, and this became the basis for his 1764 autobiography, *An Authentic Narrative*. The book soon introduced him to a wide range of readers, both at home and abroad, and John became the kind of person worth making a detour for. When the letters were published, he noticed that folks looked at him differently in the street in Olney: "The people stare at me since reading them, and well they may. I am indeed a wonder to many."

In the first weeks of winter in 1772, just weeks before William Cowper would descend in his fiercest struggle and the first traces of "Amazing Grace" would appear, John prepared to welcome a new visitor, James Albert, whose own autobiography had just been published. Like John, he had lived in Africa for some years, sailed across to America, and now made a home for himself in England. Unlike John, however, Albert—whose original name was Ukawsaw Gronniosaw—had made most of his journey as an African slave.

John was nervous before the meeting. He had sat with many opponents of slavery, but never with a former slave. He knew a little of his visitor's story, enough to reassure himself that there was no danger that he had personally been involved in this man's forced migration from his homeland to America, but there was little comfort in it. The closer the meeting came, the more shy John felt.

James Albert Ukawsaw Gronniosaw sat down and composed himself. He breathed slow and deep, just like he had been taught as a child by his father, the reigning king of the city of Bournou and all the lands beyond. Sabbath days they would rise early enough to reach their place of worship an hour before sunrise. There they remained, on their knees, hands held up, in strict silence until almost noon. After years spending every week that way, composure came easily.

He looked at the minister sitting opposite him. He did not appear to be the kind of man who would choose to sit in silence for hours on end. Barely any Englishmen ever did. But this man, in whose house James was now sitting, did have something about him that marked him out. Where most people could not stop staring at James, Newton was struggling to look at him at all.

"I was born in the city of Bournou," he began once the formal pleasantries of tea and polite conversation were concluded. "My mother was the eldest daughter of the reigning king there. I was the youngest of six children, and particularly loved by my mother, and my grandfather doted on me."

He paused. Being an author promoting his book, the words were familiar now. Sometimes they seemed to belong to someone else.

"I was a curious child, full of questions that no person could ever answer. I wanted to know who made the first lion, who makes the thunder, who made the first man. It troubled my mother that she could not answer, and it angered my father to see me upset her so. When a merchant who traded ivory with our people visited and offered to take me to the Guinea coast, where I would see white folks and houses with wings so that they could walk upon the water, it was agreed that I should go. I was given much gold—worn as chains around my neck and ankles. I was happy at first, but there were other men traveling with the merchant, and some of them spoke badly of me and wanted to throw me in a pit. The journey was more than one thousand miles, and by the time we reached the coast I was greatly troubled.

"The city we arrived at was like no other city I had ever dreamed of. There were trumpets and drums sitting on top of wooden structures taller than English steeples. Great crowds would hear the noise from miles away and gather beneath. I was in awe, but not for long. I was told that the king of the city believed me to be a spy of my father's and intended to kill me.

"On the day I was summoned, I washed my gold ornaments carefully to make them shine. I approached the king—sitting on his throne at the far end of a court lined with guards on either side for three hundred paces. He had a scimitar in his hand, ready to behead me himself, and I walked up to him with courage. His heart melted when he saw me and he announced that he would not kill me, but that I should be sold as a slave instead."

James Albert Ukawsaw Gronniosaw paused. Newton was finally looking at him, and his face was drained of color.

"Please," said his host. "Continue."

"I was taken on board a French brig, but the captain said I was too small to buy, so I was returned to the merchant. He considered me too much trouble and would have killed me himself had a Dutch trader not bought me for two yards of cloth. My new master took my gold as well, and I endeavored to serve him well. Every Sabbath day he would read from a book of prayers to the ship's crew. I was astounded and thought the book itself was talking to him. When he was finished, I pressed my own ears to the book, hoping that it would speak to me, too, but no words came.

"Once we arrived in Barbados I was sold to a man of the city of New York. He dressed me well and treated me kindly and gave me the job of waiting at his table. I was sold again, to Mr. Freelandhouse, a very gracious and good minister. He bought me and took me home with him. There he taught me to pray to God in heaven, who was my father and best friend. This troubled me and made me sad. I told him that my father was in Bournou with my mother and sister, and I would very much like to return to them. My master cried heavy tears at this. He told me that God was a great and good God who created all the world and every person living in Africa, America, and beyond. I was always at home, he told me, no matter where I was. While I was happy to hear this, it was not easy for me to find peace whenever I heard about God's wrath and judgment. I was troubled greatly, convinced of my own corrupt nature, sure that I was a sinner for whom there was no salvation."

Newton shifted in his seat and James Albert Ukawsaw Gronniosaw paused. "I think you understand what I am saying."

"I do."

"It was troubling to me until I was given a book that explained the forgiveness of Jesus for sinners like you and me. I fell to my knees when I read it, joy unspeakable taking possession of my soul. I ran to tell my master, but all comfort was suddenly blasted from my world, for dear Master Freelandhouse was dying from a fever. I took his hand in mine and told him about what I now knew about the mercy of God. He was happy and told me he had given me my freedom. From then on, he said, I was at liberty to go where I wished."

The light was fading but the story continued. James Albert Ukawsaw Gronniosaw spoke about all five of Mr. Freelandhouse's sons dying in the next four years. He talked about his time as a privateer, being swindled repeatedly and abused regularly by his fellow crewmen. He had also joined the navy for a time and, like John, had served under Admiral Sir George Pocock. They had other things in common, too, and he described hearing George Whitefield preach in New York several times and his long-held desire to one day travel to England, where he was sure every inhabitant was a holy, God-fearing believer.

"I cannot describe my joy when we were within sight of Portsmouth. But I was astonished when we landed to hear the inhabitants of that place curse and swear. I expected to find nothing but goodness, gentleness, and meekness in this Christian land."

The two men laughed a good while at that. When the story turned to love, James explained how when he first met Betty, his wife, she was a widow with a child and was in debt. Friends objected to him marrying someone so poor, but his mind was made up. He sold practically everything he owned in order to clear her debt, and he never felt happier in his life.

"We are pilgrims," he concluded after he had spoken about his hopes that by sharing his story in a book, he might be able to provide for his family. "Sometimes we are too poor to afford a fire or a candle. But God is pleased to incline the hearts of his people to help. We are pilgrims traveling through many difficulties toward our heavenly home. We wait patiently for his gracious call. One day, he shall deliver us out of this present world and bring us to the everlasting glories of the world to come."

When he had finished speaking, neither man spoke for several minutes.

"On first meeting you today," said Newton eventually. "I was . . . I was not sure what to expect. But I have never felt such gladness upon meeting a Christian brother. You have reminded me of the most powerful of truths—that God is sovereign and that God is a provider. We can trust him, can we not?"

Attitudes toward slavery were not the only shifts taking place within society, nor was the slave trade the only social ill that John cared about. England had been locked in conflict for decades, starting with the war with France that had caused him to be pressed onto the *Harwich*, and continuing with the Seven Years' War and the American War of Independence. The military was stretched, and soon after John left the slave trade, the prime minister, William Pitt, introduced conscription. Those drawn by ballot served three years in Britain as militiamen. By the time they returned home to sleepy villages like Olney, they were rough, rude, and ready to raise some hell.

John turned to the pulpit and the hymn sheet to try to turn them around:

> *Have mercy on our num'rous youth,*
> *Who young in years are old in sin;*
> *And by thy Spirit, and thy truth,*
> *Show them the state their souls are in.*

On November 5, 1777, the lads were even more rowdy than usual. A recent fire—started by accident—had destroyed twelve thatched cottages in the village, driving families further into poverty and causing the village leaders to call for the usual Guy Fawkes Day celebrations to be scaled down. Most villagers accepted the restrictions, but the former militiamen were not happy. They wanted their bonfires and their booze, and if they couldn't have one, they'd double up on the other.

Forty or fifty loud, drunk, and violent young men can make a lot of noise, especially when everyone else has retreated into their houses under the cover of darkness. They stormed through Olney, breaking windows, screaming for money, and threatening worse to come.

John heard them. He was out of bed, dressed, and downstairs before Mary could know what was going on. Lacing his boots, he could feel old muscles twitching back to life, recalling lessons learned in how to survive when death was seconds away. He was calm, his fingers moving steadily with lace and button. He knew how to deal with a mob. Identify the leader, show no fear, stand your ground, and be prepared to inflict pain.

As he reached for the door, he looked back and saw Mary. She was crying.

"It is nothing," he said. "I will quieten them."

"No!" she said, the strength of her voice surprising them both. "Please. I can see the light of their fires from the window. There are too many."

"It will not take long. I promise. I have faced worse than a herd of drunken English youth."

Mary opened her mouth to protest again, but instead of words, a deep, painful sob emerged. Soon her shoulders were shaking, her cries interrupted by deep, ragged gasps for breath.

John held her, whispering that it would be well, reminding her that God was on their side. The more he spoke, the louder she cried.

The sound of glass smashing nearby brought them both round. John kissed her on the head and went to the door.

Mary screamed.

He turned and saw her fall to the floor.

Several minutes later, after she had recovered from her fainting and he had carried her upstairs, there was a knock at the door.

"No!" Mary cried weakly as he hurried downstairs to answer it.

His conversation was brief and too quiet for her to hear.

"Polly! My dearest," he said as he returned and cradled her in his arms. "Do you hear the mob now?"

"No."

"Good. There is no need to worry. They are gone."

"How?"

John looked away. "I did not fight. I sent someone in my place to beg for peace and offer the captain of the mob a shilling to secure our protection."

John was ashamed of the way he dealt with the mob. It was cowardly and weak, exactly the kind of response that would have seen him killed while at sea. It was also yet another sign that his time at Olney was drawing to a close. The once-peaceful parish that had welcomed him with open arms had changed. A clear line had been drawn, dividing opinion on the vicar. It wasn't just the rowdy youth who had lost interest and respect. Church attendance was down, and people were starting to speak publicly against him. There were some still on his side, especially the ever-loyal William Cowper and Mary Unwin, but not nearly as many as before.

John thought that saying goodbye to Olney would mean saying goodbye to slow-brewing dissatisfaction and the chaos of violent mobs. He was mistaken. Taking up a position as rector of St. Mary Woolnoth in the city of London early in 1780, he went ahead of Mary. She arrived in time, however, for one of the worst riots in living memory. Fired up on anti-Catholic sentiment, a mob fifty-thousand strong ruled the city for almost a week at the beginning of June. With no police force in the city and troops ordered not to fire, the drunken rioters did as they pleased. They brawled in the streets, looting and burning houses of those who would not pay their ransoms. They destroyed a distillery, some looters perishing in the flames, others drinking themselves to death on the pure alcohol that leaked into the gutters. For three nights running John and Mary could see from their back windows six or seven terrible fires burning out of control. John had to write back to Olney to reassure William Cowper that no houses where they lived had been torched. Yet the violence was close enough to the Newtons' new home for John to witness firsthand acts of cruelty that were truly shocking.

London was a city divided. The West End was bathed in elegant luxury. It was the time of plunging necklines and fast-changing extravagant fashions, of men in powdered wigs and gold buckled shoes gambling away thousands of pounds in their clubs. The East End, however, sank deeper in squalor. The poor slept seventeen to a room without sanitation, knowing that either through violence or sickness, death would catch up with them sooner or later.

John had no interest in courting the favor of the wealthy but approached rich and poor alike with the same singular determination. He wanted to preach the gospel, to tell them all about the sacrifice for our sins made by Jesus on the cross. He wanted to talk about redeeming love, undeserved mercy, and amazing grace, and he was willing to use any vehicle at his disposal to do so.

His *An Authentic Narrative* had become widely known in the sixteen years since its publication. While he was still in Olney he had followed up with another book, *Twenty-Six Letters on Religious Subjects*. Again he chose to publish anonymously, under the Greek word *Omicron*, chosen because Christ was the Omega, or large *O* in Greek, but John was simply Omicron, the smaller *o*. The year before his move to London he and Cowper published *Olney Hymns*, a collection of almost 350 hymns, including "Glorious Things of Thee Are Spoken," "How Sweet the Name of Jesus Sounds," and "Amazing Grace." Another collection of letters, titled *Cardiphonia* (meaning "the utterance of the heart"), followed a year after his arrival in London. He had somehow become an author.

He seemed to have a particular gift for offering wise spiritual direction through letters. Before long, he would find in London that he was always working from a stack of some sixty unanswered letters. Folding a quarto sheet of paper neatly in half gave him a front page, two inside pages, and a back page to fill up with his graceful roundhand, line upon line, and that seemed about the right length to treat most personal spiritual concerns that came his way. Many letters he wrote were written only after he had been on his knees in prayer. He had become a spiritual director through the post. When he had enough suitable copies of his letters to hand, he would choose some to publish anonymously in magazines and others to appear in collections as general spiritual advice for readers.

Whether he was preaching at church or writing hymns, sharing his thoughts on contemporary issues in letters or reflecting on his own unique story, John shared the same aim as other spiritually awakened leaders. All such earnest Christians were called "Methodists" now by their critics, regardless of what church they attended. If that's what he was to be called, so be it. He wanted to communicate from the heart, to break through the formalities of religion and help escort people to a place where, like him, they could accept their weakness and place their trust in God alone.

At first, the parishioners of St. Mary's were unimpressed. The wealthy nodded and smiled politely enough when they swept into church, but there was little in the way of connection between them and their new rector. Yet as the months passed, and word of the new preacher spread—one of very few "awakened clergy" in the city at the time—the church filled up with curious visitors. Just like in Olney, the church built a gallery to accommodate the increase in numbers.

People were interested in John, and he took to his new life in the nation's capital. Yet the attention did not go to his head. When one of the most celebrated authors of her day, Hannah More, requested a meeting, John treated her no differently from any other person. He listened to her, reassured her in her struggles, and urged her to turn to Christ. It made a difference, and Hannah More became not just a loyal friend of John but an influential philanthropist and vocal supporter of evangelical causes.

In the final two decades of the eighteenth century, the world was in a state of political and social turmoil. The list of social problems requiring change was vast. Yet slavery was the one issue that stood out above all others, especially for the expanding network of those who shared Newton's concern for the gospel and would therefore soon be described as evangelicals. For centuries slavery had been widely accepted by the British as part of the necessary order, but now public opinion was turning. John Wesley had already published against the slave trade in 1774, and firsthand accounts of people like James Albert Ukawsaw Gronniosaw helped to raise awareness of the human suffering involved. But it would take something profoundly shocking to truly break through and impact the public conscience.

And that "something" happened in 1781. The Guinea trader *Zong* was packed tight with 470 slaves. Sickness erupted while it was on the Middle Passage, claiming the lives of sixty Africans and seven crew. Faced with such colossal losses, the captain called a meeting of the crew. He told them that if the sickness was left to run its course and the slaves died of natural causes, their profits would be slashed. If, however, the slaves died by some other means— not of natural causes but an unforeseen tragedy like being thrown alive into the sea—then the losses would be covered by the insurance that the ship's owners had taken out.

Some crew objected, but most did not.

That evening, fifty-four slaves had their hands bound and were thrown, alive, overboard.

Two days later the crew bound and threw another forty-two to the waves.

A day later, twenty-six more.

The scenes were so terrifying, so shocking, that ten slaves voluntarily jumped to their deaths without being bound or thrown.

In all, a total of 132 slaves died on the Middle Passage. When they landed in Jamaica, the captain tried to convince people that he had been forced to throw the slaves overboard because there was a lack of water, but this was a lie: the ship still contained hundreds of gallons, and nobody had been put on reduced rations.

The insurers refused to pay and the case went to court. Initially the jury sided with the crew, but the subsequent appeal—which created widespread publicity—ruled against the ship's owners. It was a landmark decision, and one that brought the horrors of the Middle Passage to the public's attention like never before. London-based opponents to the trade like Olaudah Equiano, "the African," and the antislavery campaigner Granville Sharp made sure the murders aboard the *Zong* were not forgotten. They made sure, too, that they recruited others to their cause. Women like Hannah More and men like William Wilberforce.

After John and Mary moved to London in late 1779, William Cowper's religious despair remained as entrenched as ever, but he continued to write poems, including many that critiqued the conventional morality of society. As he accumulated enough poems to consider publication, he stayed in close touch by letter with John in London and asked him in April 1781 to write a preface for the collection. The poems came off the press in 1782, just before the *Zong* massacre became public knowledge, and they had a strong ethical message about the need for true Christian faith as a foundation for reforming society. William wrote to John that his long poem "Charity" in particular was written not to be popular but to do good. He wrote of the bonds of charity that God intended should bind all humankind, but also of how far the nation had fallen:

> *But ah! what wish can prosper, or what pray'r,*
> *For merchants rich in cargoes of despair,*
> *Who drive a loathsome traffic, gauge, and span,*
> *And buy the muscles and the bones of man!*

He was mounting a public challenge to the slave trade as inhumane, and doing so with rhetorical force and emotional intensity. And he did so as a Christian:

> *Canst thou, and honour'd with a Christian name,*
> *Buy what is woman-born, and feel no shame?*
> *Trade in the blood of innocence, and plead*
> *Expedience as a warrant for the deed?*

John sat down to pen his preface for this collection in his study at Charles Square near the open fields on the edge of the city, two miles north of the church. Looking over his friend's poems one more time and saying a prayer under his breath, he knew what he wanted to tell the readers. These were serious poems from a serious person who communicated with grace his firm grasp of truth, beauty, and the influence of the Bible. It was only this that was strong enough and deep enough to reform human character and conduct.

William Wilberforce and John Newton had history. When he was just a child, William heard Newton preach, and the single encounter was enough to leave its mark. Growing up, William thought of John as a kind of spiritual father. By the time he was twenty-six years old, living in London and serving as member of Parliament for Yorkshire, he was still nervous about meeting Newton. After all, Wilberforce had earned for himself a reputation as a well-liked, convivial member of fashionable society who liked the finer things in life. It was a reputation that began to trouble him, especially when he experienced the first stirrings of a spiritual awakening as he had recently. The more he prayed and the more he read, the more he struggled to know what he should be doing with his life. Should he carry on as an MP or should he seek ordination? It was a difficult choice to make. He needed an older, wiser head to help him navigate the way forward.

On the advice of a mutual friend, Wilberforce wrote to Newton and asked if they could meet. Knowing that the rumors would fly if he was seen in the company of an evangelical preacher, he had asked that the meeting be secret. Newton agreed and invited him to his house in Hoxton three days later.

William's nerves almost got the better of him. He arrived early, patrolling the street outside, checking to see whether anyone might be watching. Only when he was sure that the way was clear did he hurry to the door and knock quickly.

Within minutes of sitting down in Newton's study, William was struck by three things.

First, that more than any other person he had ever met before, Newton radiated calm and peace.

"I had always entertained hopes and confidence that God would one day bring you to me," the old minister said as soon as he had offered William tea. With just a handful of words, William could feel all the apprehension that had been with him in the street drain away.

Second, that while Newton's sixty years were clearly etched on his face, the man was as sharp and insightful as someone half his age. "Do not become cut off from your friends," Newton added, as William spoke of his struggles trying to decide between ordination and Parliament. "It is hoped and believed that the Lord has raised you up for the good of his church, and for the good of the nation . . . I believe you are the Lord's servant and are in the post which He has assigned you; and though it appears to me to be more arduous, and requiring more self-denial than my own, I know that He who has called you to it can afford you strength according to your day."

Finally, but most surprisingly of all, Wilberforce was struck by the subject that Newton returned to again and again. Barely a half hour went by without the old man mentioning the slave trade. Every time he did, his voice trembled a little with remorse.

The following Sunday, Wilberforce approached St. Mary's. There were still some traces of nerves, especially as there was such a great crowd gathered to hear the Reverend John Newton preach. Wilberforce could tell that some people noticed him, but any unease he felt was outweighed by a far stronger force within. He was hungry to hear more of the life-changing truth.

Newton's sermon that day, December 7, 1785, was simple. He preached about the "addiction of the soul to God." William sat enraptured.

Days later William read *An Authentic Narrative,* inhaling every word.

In the new year the two men continued to meet, no longer in secret.

Months passed and their regular meetings continued. William had found in Newton a pastor and mentor of rare skill. It did not take long for the fruit to show.

It was after the two met on a Sunday at the end of October 1787 that William wrote in his diary: "God Almighty has set before me two great objects, the suppression of the slave trade and the reformation of manners."

Not long after William Wilberforce had crept into his house like a nervous animal fearful for its safety, Newton wrote a letter to William Cowper. *I hope the Lord will make him a blessing as both a Christian and a statesman. How seldom do these characters collide! But they are not incompatible.*

As well as meeting him in person, Newton wrote regularly to Wilberforce. The letters were an opportunity to clarify and reinforce the lessons he felt were particularly important for Wilberforce to learn:

> *When you first favored me with a call at Hoxton, I observed to you, that we little folks, so distant from the public circle in which you move, and so unacquainted with many circumstances belonging to it, that I thought none of us were competent to advise you; that you must be your own Casuist, or rather, I hoped and trusted, that from your attention to the Word of God, and the throne of his Grace, you would derive wisdom from the highest source and a divine light would shine upon your paths. There is none teacheth like God, but he teaches us gradually and in the school of Experience.*

Always gracious, John was willing to share his opinions, especially when it came to Wilberforce's fear of disapproval:

> *I believe the Methodists have been the instruments of much good, but their zeal has been in many instances intemperate and injudicious, the preaching and conduct of some has been enthusiastic and wild, and there have been amongst them, as will always be the case, in the visible church, pretenders, who have given just cause of offense. I am not therefore fond of bearing the name, nor do I justly*

deserve it, for I am a regular Minister of the Establishment. But as the term is indiscriminately applied to all who profess the doctrines of the Reformation, and who endeavor to walk according to the rule of the Gospel, I must not be ashamed of it; for I cannot escape it at a cheaper rate, than by renouncing or concealing my principles, and by adapting my conversation, to the prevailing taste and custom of the Age.

I conceive therefore, that an upright conscientious man, cannot by the most circumspect and prudent behavior, wholly avoid the censure and dislike of the World, so far as his religious principles are concerned, and he is determined to square his life according to the precepts and spirit of the Gospel. He must expect to be misunderstood by some, and misrepresented by others. For in a degree, and upon some occasions at least, all who will live godly in Christ Jesus must suffer persecution.

Having spent his earlier years struggling to take control of his impulses and uphold the ideals that ran deep within him, Newton knew the value of established character and was keen to encourage Wilberforce in the development of his:

But then, He may by the grace of God, attain to such an established character for Integrity, Benevolence, Meekness, Chearfulness and Consistency, as shall upon the whole counteract and shame the insinuations of gainsayers; and force a conviction upon their minds, whether they will confess it or not, that he is better than themselves. Yea, if his mind be comprehensive, and his eye single, if he be fixed in his determination to obey and please God rather than Man, in cases where it is not possible to please both—In proportion as his character is formed upon this plan, and generally known, he may compel their respect and reverence, and have an influence and weight among them, in the common affairs of life, greater than they usually have over one another.

John's words came from the heart and his wisdom was gained through experience. Like all good preachers, he was sharing wisdom that he needed for himself. He had tasted the medicine; he knew that it worked. He knew that it would continue to work. Wilberforce could stay in politics with the courage of his Christian convictions.

And so, despite his age, his recognition as a writer, and his position of respect within the growing evangelical community, John was not deaf to his own words or prone to resting on his laurels. His desire to help young Wilberforce take on his calling and influence the world around him was genuine. It was an opportunity he did not want to waste.

As he saw Wilberforce join with others to fight the slave trade, his own path was becoming clearer. He had written about his past already, but what he had shared about his involvement in the slave trade had been limited. The shocking details—the kind that, like events on the *Zong*, would both horrify people and motivate them to call for change—were nowhere to be seen in *An Authentic Narrative*. It was authentic in as much as John was scrupulous about only including the truth, but it was not complete. He had left much off the page, and he knew it. As he confessed to a friend a few years later, he had written chiefly about his misery rather than about his wickedness. If he had, "the book would have been too shocking to bear a reading."

If facing the mob in Olney had revealed to him anything, it was that he still remembered how to fight, how to steel himself, draw on his courage, and stand firm. It taught him that when he suppressed that desire to put an end to an injustice, he felt nothing but shame.

There was more to say. More to share. More to be risked. But so much more to be gained.

In the final years of the 1780s, abolitionism was quickly becoming a mass movement. There were petitions and campaigns and even rumor of Wilberforce introducing a Parliamentary bill to change the law. John continued to advise and support his young mentee. John was old by now, but his work had never felt so urgent.

Then, one day in the winter of 1788, Mary shared some unexpected news.

She had been diagnosed with a cancerous tumor in her breast. It was the size of John's fist. There was no cure, no hope of surgery. The only help the doctor could offer was rest and laudanum.

It started with twelve men gathered in a room. A printing shop in the city of London, just a stone's throw from John's church, St. Mary's. It was May 22, 1787, and the meeting marked the formation of the Committee for the Abolition of the Slave Trade. Among the twelve was Granville Sharp, the lawyer and antislavery campaigner who had helped bring news of the *Zong* to the public's attention. John was not among them, but his time would come. So, too, would William Wilberforce, whom they agreed to recruit. After all, with an ambition as bold as theirs, they needed an ally in Parliament, and Wilberforce was as influential as they came. There weren't many people in London who had not witnessed his recent transformation from fashionable socialite to passionate, eloquent statesman fired with godly zeal for righteous causes. Adding him to their ranks would be a significant boost.

Fighting the slave trade was a battle with many fronts, and the committee was aware of the need for more than just a spokesman in the House of Commons. With the wind at their backs, they needed to seize on the growing public interest in the issue. They needed to flood the public with information from sermons, pamphlets, and reports, to poems, newspaper articles, and petitions. The truth about the slave trade had been hidden from the public for centuries. By existing in secret, it had been allowed to grow and flourish. But no longer. Now it was time to remove any excuse for ignorance.

The owner of the printing shop, James Phillips, set about commissioning writers to address the subject. John Newton was an obvious choice, and by the end of January 1788 his forty-one-page essay *Thoughts on the African Slave Trade* was ready for sale at a price of one shilling. This time, unlike *Omicron* or

Cardiphonia, there was no hiding behind a pseudonym. John Newton's name was right there on the cover for all to see.

John came out swinging.

There was nothing quite so "iniquitous, so cruel, so oppressive, so destructive, as the African Slave Trade," he wrote. He called it a "disgraceful branch of commerce," a "stain of our National character." He exposed not just the loss of life among British sailors but also the way the trade corrupted them and brutalized the slaves themselves. He refuted the suggestion that Africans were in some way subhuman and wrote about their humanity. And, writing as one of the best-known preachers in the country at the time, he made it clear which side of the issue God was on. As he would write later in a private note: "If Men do not vindicate the cause of the oppressed Africans, I cannot but believe the Judge of all the Earth will take it into his own hands. My heart trembles for the Consequences."

Aware that he could easily be branded a hypocrite for preaching against the trade he once profited from, John wrote *Thoughts on the African Slave Trade* with brutal honesty: "I am bound in conscience to take shame to myself by a public confession, which, however sincere, comes too late to prevent or repair the misery and the mischief to which I have, formally been an accessory."

He explained that it would "always be a subject of humiliating reflection to me, that I was once an active instrument in a business at which my heart now shudders."

He was honest about the fact that he only quit the trade because of ill health. "I think I should have quitted it sooner, had I considered it, as I now do, to be unlawful and wrong."

He was not looking to excuse his actions but tried to explain his reasons for dedicating six years of his life to it: "I never had a scruple upon this head at the time; nor was such a thought once suggested to me by any friend. . . . What I did, I did ignorantly." As he said a few years later in another publication, "Custom, example, and interest, had blinded my eyes."

Thoughts on the African Slave Trade was welcomed by the members of the abolition committee with open arms and open wallets. They bought up all unsold copies, ordered that three thousand more be printed, and made sure that every member of both the House of Commons and the House of Lords received a copy.

The publication was influential, yet in the months following its publication, John was troubled. He had measured his words carefully as he had written the essay, but now he was second-guessing himself. He had been honest in his account of his time in the slave trade, but had he been honest enough? He had told the truth, but was it the whole truth?

John's concerns related to his time aboard the *Brownlow*, when he was first mate to Captain Richard Jackson. They were terrible days, especially in the early months when John's newfound faith had fallen away so quickly. Jackson had taken great delight in seeing his first mate stumble like he had, and the closer they got to the Guinea coast, the more determined the captain appeared to drag John down into his world of darkness—to the "hell of my own" that he was so proud to have created.

Even at the time, Jackson's cruelty was shocking. The incident with the dead body being thrown to the sharks still haunted John forty years later, all the more so when events on the *Zong* made the news. But there was more to share than that one incident on deck. There were darker memories that had been hidden deep down. Memories of conversations with Jackson that John would rather not remember, let alone share with the rest of the world.

Having struggled while he wrote *Thoughts on the African Slave Trade*, John had decided not to share the stories of his time with Jackson. Sometimes the truth was just too sickening in its brutality.

Six months later he was having doubts.

In the summer following the publication of *Thoughts on the African Slave Trade*, John sat down to write about the business of the campaign to Richard Phillips, cousin to James who had printed *Thoughts* and another one of the founding members of the Committee for the Abolition of the Slave Trade. John and Richard had been corresponding and meeting in person for years. Theirs was a friendship that was born in the days when Mary knew nothing of her tumor and the committee was yet to be established. Back then, Richard had encouraged John to write about his experiences, but John had declined, explaining that whenever he contemplated the subject, he became so overwhelmed with horror that writing would be impossible. If there was anyone whom John could trust with the whole, barbaric and unfiltered truth, it was Richard.

5th July, 1788

Dear Sir,

I have been so much engaged I can but just answer your wishes, if at all; for I am liable to interruption every moment. I think the following notes are all that I can suggest, in addition to what I have already written, if you should think it proper to reprint the pamphlets.

The perusal of Mr. Falconbridge's pamphlet, and of some others, since the publication of my own, reminds me of a particular which should have been inserted under this article. The very ill-treatment the seamen receive from the captain, or those who act under his authority, is often fatal. I have myself—and I believe more than once—seen sick men, who were unable to work, beaten or flogged, under a pretence that they were lazy, till they died under the blows. A savageness of spirit, not easily conceived, infuses itself (though, as I have observed, there are exceptions) into those who exercise power on board an African slave-ship, from the captain downwards. It is the spirit of the trade, which, like a pestilential air, is so generally infectious, that but few escape it. Many of the captains are brought up in the business; and pass through the several stages of apprentices, foremastermen, and mates, before they are masters, and gradually acquire a cruel disposition together with their knowledge of the trade: and, as it often happens that they are men of no education, and have no taste for books or turn for reflection, the chief study and amusement of their leisure hours seems to be, how to make the sailors, at least such of them as they take a dislike to, as miserable as they can. I remember one, who stood upon the quarter-deck while his vessel was casting off from the pier-head at Liverpool, and, with a suitable expression of countenance, took his leave of the people, who were standing upon the pier, with these words: "Now I have a Hell of my own!"

I have been told that I ought not to have suppressed the recital of the particulars, here referred to, out of compassion to my reader's feelings. My chief reason for suppressing it was, that it is the only instance of the kind I had knowledge of, and I would hope the only one that ever was heard of. But I submit to the respectable judgment of the friends who advised me to mention it, in case of another edition. I sailed with that captain, and therefore frequently heard the details of his cruelties from his own mouth. I do not remember the

182

whole; but two methods of his punishment of the poor slaves, whom he sentenced to die, I cannot easily forget. Some of them he jointed; that is, he cut off, with an axe, first their feet, then their legs below the knee, then their thighs; in like manner their hands, then their arms below the elbow, and then at the shoulders, till their bodies remained only like the trunk of a tree when all the branches are lopped away; and, lastly, their heads. And, as he proceeded in his operation, he threw the reeking members and heads in the midst of the bulk of the trembling slaves, who were chained upon the main-deck. He tied round the upper parts of the heads of others a small soft platted rope, which the sailors call a point, so loosely as to admit a short lever: by continuing to turn the lever, he drew the point more and more tight, till at length he forced their eyes to stand out of their heads; and when he had satiated himself with their torments, he cut their heads off. . . .

I have not time to add more than my best wishes and respects; and my prayer, that God may bless you in all things, and give you and your friends the comfort of seeing your benevolent endeavours succeed, for the suppression of that abominable trade of which I was once an abominable instrument! I hope God has forgiven me; but I ought to walk softly all my days, in the remembrance of what I have been, and what I have done.

> *I am, Sir, your sincere friend and servant,*
> *John Newton*

With no means of treating the tumor, Mary's health was declining. She disliked taking laudanum, and when she could stomach a dose, it made little impact on her pain. She spent her days in agony and her nights in sleepless turmoil. She was dying, but death was taking its time with her.

Mary's ill health was not the only crisis in the Newton home. The couple adored children, though they had never had any of their own. But in 1774, when they were still in Olney, Mary's youngest brother, George, had died. His young wife had died already, leaving a five-year-old girl, Betsy Catlett, in need of a home. John and Mary welcomed her in and brought her up as their own.

Mary's brother was not the only death in the Catlett family. Her sister,

Elizabeth, married and moved to Scotland, where Elizabeth's son died when he was twelve. A younger daughter contracted consumption and died soon after, as did her husband. Elizabeth had just one child left, Eliza, whom she sent to London to live with Mary and John in 1783. Soon after Eliza arrived, her mother died too.

The Newtons welcomed Eliza as they had welcomed Betsy. They loved their two nieces greatly and took delight in them, sharing holidays at the coasts whenever John's schedule and the girls' health allowed. Eliza had first arrived in London looking ill, and gradually her health deteriorated until she developed a fever that was a telltale sign of consumption. Eliza died in October 1785, aged fourteen. The trauma affected them all, especially Betsy, who developed a morbid fear of death. When Mary was diagnosed with breast cancer, the weight of grief at Eliza's death still hung heavy over the house.

Traumatized by her cousin's death, terrified by the sight of her aunt's visible decline in health, Betsy fell ill. She needed constant care, and between John's busyness and Mary's frailty, it was a struggle. But they persisted, prioritizing Betsy's recovery above almost every other concern.

It was against this backdrop that John was called upon to make his most significant contribution to the abolitionist cause. The first move in a campaign that was designed to run for years was for the public to hear from eyewitnesses of the brutality of the trade. John's essay on the slave trade had played a part in that process, but the message needed to reach a wider audience.

Wilberforce gave notice that he would introduce a motion in early 1788 for the abolition of the slave trade. He had been working hard to persuade Prime Minister William Pitt to launch a Parliamentary inquiry into the slave trade, knowing that if Parliament was ever going to change the law, it would need to have been exposed to the horrific truth about the trade. But Wilberforce was under enormous pressure and his body couldn't keep up. He was incapacitated for several months with an illness serious enough that he thought he might die. His motion in the House would have to wait until the following year. Still, Pitt took the important step in 1788 of launching the investigation, empowering the Privy Council and the House of Commons each to impanel witnesses and gather evidence. It was obvious who one of the star witnesses would be.

On March 28, 1789, the Reverend John Newton said a quiet goodbye to Mary, checked to make sure that Betsy was quite well, and gently shut the front door behind him. He walked south, passing coffee shops and taverns, down narrow alleys and lanes that were as familiar to him now as they were when he was a boy. He paused at church, St. Mary's. His church was perfectly silent inside, and the air was so much colder than it was on the streets. He prayed, breathed in and out—drawing strength for what was to come.

Outside again he continued his journey south, skirting past St. Paul's Cathedral and on toward the Thames. John felt tranquil as he approached the water, even though the river trade was even busier than it had been when he was a boy. People whose lives had begun in Africa or the Indies—east or west—were no longer thought of as exotic or unusual. They were part of the fabric of London, a tapestry of race, woven by trade.

He turned north just before the Palace of Westminster, crossed St. James's Park, and headed for the brick arches of St. James's Palace.

He was shown to a vast corridor outside one of the state rooms and told to wait. The ceilings were high, and distant noises echoed off the stone walls. He ignored the distractions and carried on praying. With this much at stake, the only thing he could do was rely on God to see him through.

Minutes passed and still John sat in silence. A door opened nearby and he was aware of his name being called, but he was too lost in prayer to really notice.

The voice was closer when it called his name again. He looked up and was immediately startled.

"Mr. Pitt," he said, getting to his feet, more than a little flustered. "Prime Minister, I apologize."

Pitt held out his hand and shook John's warmly. "Mr. Newton, you are most very welcome here today."

John followed the prime minister through the heavy doors and into a room big enough to house the congregations of both St. Mary's and the church at Olney and still have room for more. There were people there already—a dozen or two, rather than hundreds—gathered behind a row of tables at the far end of the room. Some of them he recognized, some he did not. Every one of them was standing and looking at him. Some were smiling, some were not.

John was shown to a chair and table that had been set apart, facing the crowd. He sat, feeling less like a captain taking charge of his ship and more like a man pressed into service. Not that he was reluctant to be there. He was glad to be able to appear before the Privy Council like this. But like his first hours on the *Harwich*, he had little idea of what he was about to face.

The questions started immediately, and they came one after another, like waves crashing against a ship.

"How long have you been resident on the coast of Africa? In what year or years? In what capacity and in what part? How long have you been in the slave trade?"

John steadied himself and answered each in turn, as it became clear that he would be cross-examined rigorously like a witness in a courtroom. After explaining that he lived in Africa for eighteen months, commanded three slave ships, and left the trade for good in 1754, he settled in, answering their questions in detail about local culture, religion, and economic life among the Sherbro people where he had lived and traded.

But then the questions pressed deeper, asking what he knew of the treatment of slaves and the moral character of the African people he met on the Windward Coast. John confessed that he had himself purchased many hundreds of slaves. It was painful to remember. He explained how these slaves were made captives through war, punishment, and kidnapping, and then how they were passed along until they reached the coast.

"And how, Mr. Newton, did the conditions for these slaves while in Africa compare to their conditions under Europeans?"

It was many years ago, but he could remember it like yesterday. "Let no one be mistaken. The situation of slaves at home is bad; worse on board the ships; and worst of all in our islands."

"What did you think of the character of the various African people you encountered?"

He drew in a deep breath, knowing this was an important question. Too many dismissed Africans as savages. All eyes were on him. "The people are gentle," he said clearly, pausing for a moment before adding, "*when* they have no communication with the Europeans." It was the slave trade that just made everyone involved incomparably worse.

He had done his best. When the report was issued the next month, it was 850 pages. And then on May 12, Wilberforce was back and, armed with evidence, he launched into a closely argued speech of three and a half hours in the House. The parliamentary campaign had begun.

The fight was far from over, however. Fifteen months later John was back, appearing this time before a House Select Committee, and the atmosphere was tense.

"Were you ever in Africa?"

John cleared his throat, leaned forward, and spoke as loud and clear as he could. "I have been in Africa." His voice echoed.

"How long ago and in what capacity?"

"I was last in Africa in 1754; I was the master of a ship in the African slave trade."

"How many voyages on the whole did you make to the coast of Africa?"

"Five."

More questions followed about the coast and the systems of governance in place among the local people. It was not difficult for John to talk about what he had observed there, especially the parts of society that he admired. As his nerves began to subside, John's answers grew. Until he checked himself. He was a preacher who knew little of politics, and here he was telling politicians about a form of government completely removed from their own. All this talking so freely risked landing him in trouble.

"After so long an interval from the year 1754," he said, the nerves returning, "I cannot be supposed to speak with equal precision or certainty; but many facts are so deeply impressed upon my mind, that I cannot forget them."

The table opposite sat in silence. All eyes returned to John.

"Is the committee to understand then, that this long interval will cause you to be uncertain in the information you shall give?"

John took their gentle rebuke and reassured them that he would do his best and always speak the truth.

The first hurdle cleared, the questions intensified.

The committee wanted to know what John thought about the people themselves and how they compared with Europeans. John found himself on firmer ground and told them exactly what he thought, no matter how shocking some might find it.

"I always judged that, with equal advantages, they would be equal to ourselves in point of capacity. . . . The people at Sherbro are in a degree civilized, often friendly, and may be trusted where they have not been previously deceived by Europeans. I have lived in peace and safety amongst them, when I have been the only white man amongst them for a great distance. The most human and moral people I ever met in Africa . . . were the people who had the least intercourse with Europe at the time."

John set about dispelling myths: Most Africans did not endorse the trade. They were not naturally lazy. Their contact with Europeans did not civilize them but instead dragged them to the lowest levels of corruption.

When the subject turned to the impact on the European sailors, John remembered the words he had written to Richard Phillips.

"The real or supposed necessity of treating the negroes with rigor gradually brings a numbness upon the heart, and renders most of those who are engaged in it too indifferent to the sufferings of their fellow-creatures. . . . There is no trade in which seamen are treated with so little humanity as in the African slave trade. I have myself seen them when sick, beaten for being lazy till they have died under the blows."

The hearing resumed the next day. The questions soon turned to the Middle Passage, the subject that occupied so much of John's mind ever since he wrote *Thoughts on the African Slave Trade*. The subject that had the greatest potential to shock and change public opinion. The subject that showed him at his worst.

"Were they chained?"

"Always," John said. "I never put them out of irons till we saw the land in the West Indies."

"Were the slaves, during the Middle Passage, in a situation of tolerable comfort when below?"

"They were rather more tolerable in my ship, because I never completed my purchase, so that they had more room; but the situation of a slave in a full ship is uncomfortable indeed."

"In what respect?"

"Their being kept constantly in irons; crowded in their lodging; and often in bad weather, almost destitute of air to breathe; besides what they suffer from the ship's motion in their irons, and the difficulty at night of getting to their tubs, which are sometimes overset."

"In cases of plots to rise, what were the punishments usually inflicted on the slaves?"

"Most generally severe floggings, to which some commanders added thumbscrews; I mean commanders of ships that I have been on board of. A captain has told me himself repeatedly, that he punished negroes after an insurrection with death."

John waited for the question to come, for him to have to explain what Captain Jackson had said about killing slaves with an axe. But the question did not come.

Instead, the focus changed. The committee wanted to know about the women and whether they suffered at the hands of the crew. John told them that they did.

The committee asked whether he had ever seen a slave chained to a dead body when the hold was checked in the morning. He told them he had seen it happen often.

Then, like a new wind striking up from the north, the subject shifted. The air grew colder. The silence more painful.

"Had you on board any of your ships any . . . children?"

He told them that he had. "About a fourth of the cargo."

"In selling the cargo, was any care taken to prevent the separation of relations?"

John heard the screams of desperate mothers piercing the sound of chaos on deck as the scramble took place. He saw the faces of terrified children as they were bundled into boats. Felt the weight of the pen in his hands as he added up the profits at the end of the day.

"It was never thought of," John said. "They were separated as sheep and lambs are separated by the butcher."

It did not take long for the hearings of the select committee to be transcribed and published. John's testimony was included along with six other witnesses who had all played a part in the slave trade. As he sat down and prepared to read the minutes, he took out his pen and wrote his name on the title page of his personal copy. This was his story, and he needed to own it.

He reached for his pen again once he finished reading his testimony.

"I make no apology for speaking publicly against this trade," he wrote. "I dare not. Should I be silent; my Conscience would speak loudly, knowing what I know. Nor could I expect a blessing on my Ministry—tho' I should speak of the sufferings of Jesus, till I was hoarse."

Finally, he added one more note.

"And he said, What hast thou done? the voice of thy brother's blood crieth unto me from the ground" (Gen. 4:10).

As soon as the hearings were over, John returned all his attention to Mary. In just a few months her condition had deteriorated significantly, especially when the summer faded and the fall set in. As soon as October began, she became fearful of what awaited her after death. She doubted her salvation and refused to talk about death at all.

The fear passed after a few weeks, but her condition continued to decline. She was too weak to get out of bed and too racked with pain to sleep. Yet on Sunday, December 12, 1790, she was well enough to celebrate a special anniversary. It was forty-eight years to the day since she and John first met at her family's home in Chatham—the day when the impetuous, tongue-tied youth fell head over heels in love with the wide-eyed girl of fourteen who was too shy to speak. Now, as man and wife, they again sat in silence, only it was not nerves that held their tongues. They had said all that needed to be said. After holding hands a while, it was almost time for John to leave for church. He prayed by her bed, they both cried, and he said goodbye.

When John returned from preaching, Mary was still alive. She was too weak to talk, but she could wave her hand at him. That was enough.

The following Wednesday, Mary was groaning, her body twitching with violent convulsions. John sat at her bedside for hours, talking, praying, holding her hand, and sitting in silence, listening to the only woman he had ever loved struggle to breathe.

In the early evening, he wrote a quick note to the doctor, updating him on her condition. "I hope her sufferings will soon be over," he wrote. "But the Lord's hour and minutes must be the best."

That night, just before 10:00 p.m., she died.

T he world seemed to die with Mary. John was distraught, and his grief grew heavy within him. He traveled down dark paths, hoping that death would take him soon or berating himself for loving his wife so much that she had become something of an idol. But grief passed. His congregation needed him. Betsy needed him. Soon he was able to return to the pulpit and preach from a text he had never previously taught on. It was Habakkuk 3:17–18: "Although the fig tree shall not blossom, neither shall fruit be in the vines . . . and the fields shall yield no meat . . . yet I will rejoice in the LORD."

Gratitude flowed naturally from John, especially when it came to his wife. He added a new ritual to his life, celebrating the anniversaries of their marriage and her birthday by writing down all that Mary had meant to him. He wrote hymns about her and read through the stack of correspondence that he had sent Mary while he was at sea, publishing them as *Letters to a Wife* in 1793. Mary was gone, but she was far from forgotten.

In spite of grief, John's instincts as a pastor remained strong. Ever since moving to London, he had been taking regular visits from young ministers and those considering the ministry. Even as late as 1797 he was still opening his doors on Tuesdays and Saturdays, sometimes having as many as forty visitors each day.

Many people hung on his every word as they sat around his breakfast table or in his smoke-filled study. They smiled at his wit and enjoyed his humor, but it was his humility and his integrity that left the deepest impressions. John was a larger-than-life character, a well-known preacher and writer and leader within the church. But he had little time for wielding influence on a national stage, or for strong-arming others to do as he said. "I am not very fond either of assemblies, consistories, synods, councils, benches, or boards," he wrote later on in his life. "Thus there are ten or a dozen of us in London, who frequently meet; we deliberate, ask, and give advice as occasions arise; but the sentiment of one, or even of the whole body, is not binding upon any." Yet his influence in these informal gatherings would shape a whole generation of Christian leaders.

In the years following Mary's death, Betsy cared for her uncle. She read to him when his eyesight failed and accompanied him on his walks. But her own health was fragile, and she had never fully recovered from the death of her cousin, Eliza. Fear of death stalked her constantly, and a decade after Mary's death, Betsy suffered a nervous breakdown. She was committed to the infamous Bethlem Hospital—more commonly known as Bedlam—a place where many healthy people were held in chains, never to leave. The mentally ill were treated as inmates and viewed as a spectacle.

John's time on Plantain Island had taught him what it was like to be trapped, overwhelmed, and fearful. It was not something to face alone. So every day that Betsy was in Bedlam, John had a servant guide him to the hospital's perimeter. He would wave a white handkerchief in the direction of Betsy's window and wait until his companion confirmed that she was waving back. In the year that she was incarcerated, he never missed a day.

Betsy's health recovered and she returned home, marrying a local optician who moved in with her and John. They were good years, times that John described as "heart-peace, house-peace, and church-peace."

John grew old and weak. His eyes became too feeble to write, and his memory began to fail. "What do I do here?" he called out when he got confused midway through a marriage service.

His friends were concerned.

"You have been a long voyage, and are now entering into port," wrote one. "If the voyage is nearly finishing, may you enter into port with swelling sails, and the softest, sweetest gales."

John did not take the hint. He continued preaching as he turned eighty. He bumbled on, frequently losing his train of thought while preaching. Removing him from the pulpit was an impossible task.

"I cannot stop," he yelled as a visitor suggested that his time was up. "Shall the old African blasphemer stop while he can still speak?"

Gradually, John's firebrand will and determination started to lose in the battle with his body. He preached his last sermon in October 1806, and by the following January he was unable to walk. He was confined to his bed, where Betsy and her husband would take turns reading to him from the Bible.

"I am like a person going on a journey in a stagecoach, who expects its arrival every hour," he said to one friend in his final year.

"Packed and sealed and waiting for the post," he said to another.

Another time, he reflected that in the face of death, he hoped he might retire "as a thankful guest from a full table."

It was springtime when Wilberforce's bill passed, banning British ships from playing any part in the slave trade.

It was winter when John entered his final days.

John Newton lay in the fading light. He was perfectly still. The journey was nearly over. The work almost complete. His eyesight was failing, but his vision was perfectly clear. He knew the wretch that he had once been. He knew where he was heading. And he knew who was taking him there.

"My memory is nearly gone," he said to a friend before he died. "But I remember two things: that I am a great sinner, and that Christ is a great Savior."

L ike John Newton himself, the slave trade did not die quickly.

At first, in the late 1780s, it had appeared as though the fight for the abolition of the slave trade would be won swiftly, thanks to apparently successful Privy Council and House Select Committee hearings. Yet the parliamentary bill that Wilberforce introduced immediately afterward was defeated by 163 votes to 88. After three hundred years of profit, those who had built their fortunes upon the trade in human cargo were unwilling to give up without a fight.

Each year Wilberforce introduced a bill to abolish the trade, and each year it was defeated. Those who voted against Wilberforce pointed first to the turmoil in France following the Revolution, and then to the carnage and bloodshed in Haiti, when the slaves rose up and threw aside their colonial masters. Pitt lost interest in abolition, the monarchy directly opposed it, and throughout the 1790s the campaign that had enjoyed such momentum a decade before appeared to be stalling.

With his life's work in tatters, Wilberforce was sickened by the fact that instead of declining, the slave trade appeared to be thriving. Yet, in 1804, the tide started to turn. His bill finally passed in the House of Commons, though it was too late to be passed in the House of Lords. Three years later, the Abolition of the Slave Trade Act finally passed and received royal assent—just nine months before John Newton died on December 21, 1807. The act was a significant success, but not a complete victory. The bill only stopped British ships from taking part in the trade. It would take until July 26, 1833, for slavery itself to be abolished and for those it had held captive to be emancipated.

Three days later, Wilberforce died.

I. CHRONICLES.

HYMN XLI.

Faith's review and expectation.
Chap. xvii. 16, 17.

1 AMazing grace! (how sweet the sound)
    That sav'd a wretch like me!
I once was lost, but now am found,
    Was blind, but now I see.

2 'Twas grace that taught my heart to fear,
    And grace my fears reliev'd;
How precious did that grace appear,
    The hour I first believ'd!

3 Thro' many dangers, toils and snares,
    I have already come;
'Tis grace has brought me safe thus far,
    And grace will lead me home.

4 The LORD has promis'd good to me,
    His word my hope secures;
He will my shield and portion be,
    As long as life endures.

5 Yes, when this flesh and heart shall fail,
    And mortal life shall cease;
I shall possess, within the vail,
    A life of joy and peace.

6 The earth shall soon dissolve like snow,
    The sun forbear to shine;
But GOD, who call'd me here below,
    Will be for ever mine.

The Original Text of "Amazing Grace"

At eighty years of age, John Newton penned with a shaky hand the very last entry in his diary. It was March 21, 1805, the anniversary of the violent North Atlantic storm in 1748 that led to his first cry to God for mercy. He wrote, "Not well able to write. But I endeavour to observe the return of this day with humiliation, prayer, and praise."

Like this diary entry, "Amazing Grace" was itself a hymn of looking back over life's journey: "Grace has brought me safe thus far, and grace will lead me home."

What about us? Are there notes of "humiliation, prayer, and praise" for us to consider in our own lives?

We can each experience the grace of God more deeply by taking to heart four profound truths evident in Newton's story.

I can be forgiven.

Newton often turned to Psalm 130 in his meditations. It begins, "Out of the depths I cry to you, O Lord!" (esv). It was an image of the depths of the sea. In Latin, *De profundis*—out of the profound places. So, to paraphrase, "From the depths of misery, no matter how deep, I cry to the depths of mercy. From the very deepest, hardest places, I cry out. Where else can I turn?" Verse 4 of this psalm says simply, "With you there is forgiveness, that you may be feared" (esv). In Newton's words, "'Twas grace that taught my heart to fear, and grace my fears relieved."

Whatever shame or guilt you carry, however deep the regrets in your life, no matter what you have done, there is a mercy that is deeper yet. "With you there is forgiveness," said the psalmist. The psalm ends with two more affirmations: "With the LORD there is steadfast love, and with him is plentiful redemption" (v. 7 ESV). It is only in these depths of divine mercy that any of us can face our failures and disappointments. For all the beauty of the world and the goodness of human life, there is a wretchedness still to reckon with.

There were things that happened to Newton that made him wretched—the death of his mother while he was young, impressment into the brutal world of the navy, physical and psychological abuse from Evans and P. I.—but harder yet was the wretchedness he brought on himself by sheer ignorance, foolishness, and depravity. When he was in the midst of the storm and looking in the face of death, his one question was, "What mercy can there be for me?" Perhaps you have asked that question. Newton found he had to come to a place of self-despairing faith, to cry out from the depths. "I durst make no more resolves, but cast myself before the Lord, to do with me as he should please." It was like the alcoholic who has to reach bottom and let go. But then Newton found he could turn to Christ afresh, to hope and believe in a crucified Savior. "The burden," he said, "was removed from my conscience."

I can be deceived.

Secondly, though, from Newton's story we need to affirm the more frightening truth that we can be deeply self-deceived. The prophet Jeremiah accused God's people, "On your skirts is found the lifeblood of the guiltless poor. . . . Yet in spite of all these things you say, 'I am innocent'" (Jer. 2:34–35 ESV). This leads him to the conclusion, "The heart is deceitful above all things, and desperately sick; who can understand it?" (Jer. 17:9 ESV).

One of the most painful things to contemplate in Newton's story is the way he could be blind—even after his initial conversion—to his participation in race-based chattel slavery and the brutality of the forced migration of enslaved people in the most inhumane and cruel conditions. It was one thing for polite Europeans to put sugar in their tea and not realize the horrific suffering of the plantation system and the whole bloody supply chain that made this possible. It was another for someone like Newton to choose to be a part of it, enforcing it firsthand and profiting from the trade in human flesh.

According to his logbook, he bought and imprisoned 468 African men, women, and children on board his ships. Sixty-eight of those people died on his watch, while the rest he delivered into the deadly slave system that powered the plantations of the West Indies. He did this while simultaneously taking the first steps to place his personal faith in Christ. This blood was on his hands, and it took years before he became aware how self-deceived he was. "Custom, example, and interest," he wrote later, "had blinded my eyes. I did it ignorantly."

Could this happen to us? It would be naive to think it couldn't. If something is accepted by everyone (custom), and everyone else is doing it (example), and it is to my benefit (interest), then we, too, are in danger of self-deception. There are so many examples in history of good people swept up in prejudice and then conspiring in evil. One thinks of Germany in the 1930s under Hitler. But that is only the most famous example. Majorities routinely oppress minorities and tell themselves convincing lies to justify this. Dehumanization is always a first step toward violence.

For Newton and Cowper and their friends in the 1780s, the potent Christian conviction that had been lost and needed to be recovered was the universal dignity, significance, and worth of every human being, made in God's image and redeemed by an incarnate Savior who embraced all human flesh—including especially the weak and the vulnerable.

In the same poem where Cowper first condemned slavery in 1782, he laid these foundations firmly:

> He made at first, though free and unconfin'd,
> One man the common father of the kind,
> That ev'ry tribe, though plac'd as he sees best,
> Where seas or deserts part them from the rest,
> Diff'ring in language, manners, or in face,
> Might feel themselves allied to all the race.

There is one common humanity, and we are all in Adam. But we are all likewise in Christ, and we are to see human beings universally affirmed in him:

To look at him, who form'd us and redeem'd,
So glorious now, though once too disesteem'd,
. . . .
Like him, the soul thus kindled from above,
Spreads wide her arms of universal love,
And still enlarg'd as she receives the grace,
Includes creation in her close embrace.

Christ formed us and redeemed us, and now he "kindles" us to universal love. These Christian convictions were some of the most important sources for overturning prejudice and upholding equality.

It is perhaps one of the most amazing things about God's grace in the cross of Christ—that though the message of grace comes to us with impure hands, stained with violence, it yet offers hope and redemption to the wretched, and it plants the seeds of justice, reconciliation, and healing for all peoples in its universality and affirmation of the common humanity and dignity of every person.

I can make amends.

We can learn, thirdly, from Newton's story that it is possible to become undeceived, even if it happens slowly and in stages, and then we must face up to the truth, repudiate what we once believed, and do what we can, however costly, to make amends.

When Newton wrote "Amazing Grace," he was thinking of the mercy shown to King David in the Old Testament, someone whose adulterous and murderous past should have disqualified him from sharing in any of the promises of God. David's prayer of contrition was Psalm 51, where he pleaded for divine forgiveness, asked for a clean heart, and trusted that "a broken and contrite heart, O God, you will not despise" (v. 17 ESV).

Newton reckoned with his blasphemous and adulterous past long before he reckoned with the iniquity of his racism and human trafficking. But as the evil of the slave trade became more evident to him—as it did to others in Britain around the same time—he began to take a stand against the whole slave system and to make critical contributions to destroy it altogether. We have seen how he was increasingly allied with anti-slavery advocates, and we have witnessed his efforts—in private with people like Wilberforce, and in public through his writings, preaching, and legal testimony in the late 1780s and 1790s.

Once you can see the truth, you must find the courage to act.

I can be more like Jesus.

Lastly, Newton's story encourages us that God's grace changes us over our lifespan to make us more like Christ. We need grace all the way to the end, and we will never be entirely undeceived. But the closer we get to the burning radiance of Christ, the more we are exposed to the light and salted with fire.

Newton described grace as something that grows in a believer's life over time. Conversion is not "one and done." He described someone growing in grace this way: "He knows, that his heart is 'deceitful and desperately wicked;' but he does not, he cannot know at first, the full meaning of that expression." Over time there is a real change. "Much has been forgiven him, therefore he loves much, and therefore he knows how to forgive and to pity others."

He continued, "The Lord has been long teaching him this lesson by a train of dispensations; and through grace he can say, He has not suffered so many things in vain. His heart has deceived him so often, that he is now in a good measure weaned from trusting to it. . . . He is now taught to go to the Lord at once for 'grace to help in every time of need.' Thus he is strong, not in himself, but in the grace that is in Christ Jesus."

In Newton's own life we can witness this transformation. He was a changed man by the time he wrote his autobiography, and God's grace had made all the difference. In his ministry of some fifty years, we can see the power of the Holy Spirit working through him to change many hearts, to break down barriers between denominations, to build up the church with edifying writings, to nurture the spiritual growth of those training for the ministry, to encourage pioneer missionaries, to found religious societies of lasting influence, to provide apt spiritual counsel in person and by letter, and to extend compassion where others would condemn and judge. His transformed character had been evident for decades, not just at the end of his life.

Yet there was a genuine gentleness, tenderness, and humility in Newton that was, if anything, even more profound at the end of his life. As he said to Richard Phillips, "I hope God has forgiven me; but I ought to walk softly all my days, in the remembrance of what I have been, and what I have done."

When Newton thought of grace maturing in our lives, his sense was that it tended in this direction, producing a wisdom that is "first pure, then peaceable, gentle, open to reason, full of mercy and good fruits, impartial and sincere. And a harvest of righteousness is sown in peace by those who make peace" (James 3:17–18 ESV).

Grace produces the sort of people, therefore, that are not easily caught up in "a fierce contention for names, notions and parties," as Newton once wrote. In our increasingly polarized world, this is a good reminder that grace can work in us a kind of tenderness of spirit that makes for peace. Mercy triumphs over judgment. In a world of injustice, there is only so far that critique can go before it descends into recrimination, retribution, and revenge. The very universality of the hymn "Amazing Grace" suggests there is a better way, a deeper well to draw from. As the book of Hebrews says, "the sprinkled blood that speaks a better word than the blood of Abel" (12:24 ESV). It is the word of God's amazing grace in Christ Jesus.

That "better word" has echoed down the centuries and across the continents in the song that John Newton left us. It continues to speak a "better word" today.

Acknowledgments

I t is fitting for a book entitled *Amazing Grace* to acknowledge the kindness and grace that we have experienced from so many in the writing of this book. We are grateful to the many biographers who have written of John Newton's life over more than two centuries since his death in 1807—from Richard Cecil to Bernard Martin to Jonathan Aitken. We have learned from these and many others, benefiting from the continuing research that has corrected mistakes and added detail to Newton's original autobiography. We have tried to acknowledge something of our debt to previous writers in our notes on sources at the end of this book. We stand in a long line of biographers, taking our own approach in retelling Newton's story for another generation, but we are very conscious that we could not have written this book without the contribution of others.

We would like to acknowledge in particular our debt to the remarkable work of Marylynn Rouse, who has been a student of the life of John Newton for decades, transcribing manuscripts and collating sources with great care and attention. She has generously made her work available to us, as to other scholars, as well as for the edification of all who would benefit from Newton's ministry and message today. It is a rare scholar who gives so freely of all she has learned, and we want to pay tribute both to her work and her largesse. We will certainly have made our own mistakes in our retelling of John Newton's story, but the mistakes are fewer because of Marylynn.

One of the most precious gifts in life is the gift of friendship, and it has been a grace for us to collaborate on this book. It was born out of friendship, worked out over long walks in the forest, leisurely conversations around various dinner tables, and a continuous chain of email messages that linked us for much of the year, as we each woke up in turn to read what the other had written eight time zones away.

This friendship extended to include our spouses, Bruce's wife, Carolyn, and Craig's wife, Emma, and we could not have written his book without their love and support. Their grace continues to amaze us.

The team at HarperCollins have been wonderful to work with at every stage. Don Jacobson, Damon Reiss, and Kyle Olund all caught the vision when plans were still vague, and Kyle's steady guidance throughout has been invaluable. Rachel Buller has edited with kindness and care, and we are continually thankful for the skills of Katherine Hudencial, Allison Carter, and Caren Wolfe as they spread the word in ways that we cannot. Without the wonderful talents of Dave Schroeder at WTA, ably assisted by Jenaye Merida, this book would not have found its home at HarperCollins, and we are grateful that Dave has become not just an agent, but a friend as well.

The book is dedicated to Charles Morris, the president of Haven Ministries. It was Charles who thought this book should be written and who brought us together to write it. He felt in his bones that John Newton's story needed to be told, and that more people needed to hear his message of grace—now more than ever. He was right. Charles is a dear friend, and we want to honor his lifetime of faithful Christian service and public ministry. John Newton would surely have found in him a kindred spirit.

Notes

Preface

The singing of "Amazing Grace" after the tragedy of Swissair flight 111 is recounted in Kevin Cox, "Tidings of Comfort," *Homemaker's* (Nov/Dec 1998). Other accounts are reported in Mary Rourke and Emily Gwathmey, *Amazing Grace in America: Our Spiritual National Anthem* (1996), Steve Turner, *Amazing Grace: The Story of America's Most Beloved Song* (2002), and Bruce Hindmarsh, "'Amazing Grace, How Sweet It Has Sounded': The History of a Hymn and a Cultural Icon," in *Sing Them Over Again to Me: Hymns and Hymnbooks in America*, ed. by Noll and Blumhofer (2006). In addition to archival internet sources of news of "Amazing Grace" sung at times of tragedy, there are accounts in film, such as *Amazing Grace with Bill Moyers*, PBS video (1990), with excerpts at https://billmoyers.com/content/amazing-grace-bill-moyers, and BBC's Easter program, "Amazing Grace: The True Story of the Song" (broadcast April 3, 2007). In radio, there is BBC's *Soul Music* (broadcast September 18, 2001) and "The Story Behind the Song Amazing Grace," produced by Mary Weans for *This Morning: Hour One* (broadcast February 27, 2000) by Canadian Broadcasting Corporation.

Chapter 1

Most of what we know of Newton's childhood comes from his own autobiography, *An Authentic Narrative* (1764), (reprinted in *The Life and Spirituality of John Newton*, ed. Bruce Hindmarsh [2003]) and from hints in his collected works, especially his letters. Newton's autobiography was written as a series of letters to the clergyman Thomas Haweis, but there is also, in manuscript at the Morgan Library in New York, an earlier version of his narrative written as a shorter series of letters in 1762 to the Presbyterian pastor Benjamin Fawcett. This manuscript provides more details of Newton's story, and we have consulted it throughout. See also the first biography of Newton, Richard Cecil, *The Life of John Newton* (1808), which has been carefully edited by Marylynn Rouse (2000) with added material from her own extensive research. We have filled in the outline Newton gives us with some research on the social history of eighteenth-century London. See, for example, the sources at "London Lives, 1690–1800" at https://www.londonlives.org and "Landmarks in London History" at https://landmarksinlondonhistory.wordpress.com, and also the detailed maps of the city in Newton's time at "Locating London's Past" with its brilliant reproduction of John Rocque's map of the city in 1746 (https://www.locatinglondon.org/). The Museum of London has also published a small introduction by Nichola Johnson, *Eighteenth-Century London* (1991).

Chapter 2

The sources for this chapter on Newton's adolescence are the same as the last chapter, and we continue to fill in the narrative based on the account he gives us in his autobiography, including his detailed account of the vivid dream about the ring. The dialogue with his father and the Catlett family are reimagined based on the details he provides. Marylynn Rouse provides the best account of what we know of the Catlett family in her edition of Cecil, *Life of Newton* (2000). The background of mounting international tension and impending war is described in chapter 6 of Jeremy Black, *Warfare in the Eighteenth Century* (1999).

Chapter 3

We learn a little about Newton's father (also named John Newton) from Joan Craig, "Newton, John (1741–1770)," in *Dictionary of Canadian Biography* (2003), and about the Royal African Company from William A. Pettigrew,

Freedom's Debt: The Royal African Company and the Politics of the Atlantic Slave Trade, 1672–1752 (2013), but for the difficult but important relationship between father and son, we depend upon the autobiographical references from the latter. Based upon these sources, we have recreated a dialogue between the two and imagined the point of view of each of them as the historical events of the young John Newton's life unfold. The experience of being impressed into the British navy is analyzed more generally in Denver Brunsman, *The Evil Necessity: British Naval Impressment in the Eighteenth-Century Atlantic World* (2013). The details of the *Harwich* as a man-of-war are available on the web page, "British Fourth Rate ship of the line 'Harwich' (1743)" at https://threedecks.org, along with biographical details for Admiral Henry Medley (1687–1747) and Captain Philip Carteret (d. 1748). Ephraim Chambers's *Cyclopædia* (1728) provides a detailed schematic of a comparable ship in volume 2, under the entry for "ship." (View online at https://search.library.wisc.edu/digital/A4C5AV6Q7LZ5DY8E.) The correspondence between John and Mary ("Polly") is quoted at length in Bernard Martin, *John Newton: A Biography* (1950).

Chapter 4

Steve Turner suggested in his book *Amazing Grace* (2002) that when Newton was exchanged by the navy for a sailor on a Guinea slave ship in May 1745, it could not have been the *Pegasus* (under the supposed command of Captain Penrose) that he boarded, as often previously stated, but it was more likely the *Levant* under the command of James Phelps. And then, after Phelps's death, the *Levant* would have been commanded by first mate William Miller. This can be confirmed by comparing Newton's account with the data in the massive online database *Slave Voyages* at https://www.slavevoyages.org/voyage/database and the sources in David Richardson, ed., *Bristol, Africa and the Eighteenth-Century Slave Trade to America, Vol. 2: The Years of Ascendancy 1730–1745* (1987), 143. Newton describes Phelps in his manuscript autobiography as an acquaintance of his father's. When Newton left the navy, he became a common sailor, and the experience generally of a sailor in the merchant marine is described in Peter Earle, *Sailors: English Merchant Seamen, 1650–1775* (1998) and Marcus Rediker, *Between the Devil and the Deep Blue Sea: Merchant Seamen, Pirates and the Anglo-American Maritime World, 1700–1750* (2010). The identity of the part-owner of the ship who would later figure largely as Newton's master at the slave factory on Plantain Island has often been assumed to be Amos Clow. This also needs to be corrected. The version of Newton's autobiography in manuscript names this person as Evans (no first name given). These errors—the name of the ship and the name of the slave factor—both crept into the historical record from invented names in the biographical novel by Grace Irwin, *Servant of Slaves* (1961). The fitting out of a slave ship is described by Newton in his later logbook *The Journal of a Slave Trader (John Newton) 1750–1754*, ed. Martin and Spurrell (1962), and the best account of a slave ship in general is Marcus Rediker, *The Slave Ship: A Human History* (2008). When Newton becomes apprenticed to Evans and subject to P. I. at the slave "factory" on Plantain Island, we follow his own account, but we have also consulted the ethnography of the Sherbro peoples from original sources such as the observations of Nicholas Owen, *Journal of A Slave-Dealer*, ed. Eveline Martin (2016), and the tremendous research done by a descendant of one of Newton's contacts from this period: Peter L. Tucker, *The Tuckers of Sierra Leone, 1665–1914* (privately printed, 1997).

Chapter 5

We continue to draw on the same sources here as in the last chapter. The name of the new trader at Plantain Island and Kittam to whom Newton became apprenticed is not known for certain, but a plausible case has been made by Turner, *Amazing Grace* (2002) that it could be the Patrick Clow named later in Newton's logbook, and so we have used this name. There are various maps available online of the coast of West Africa in this period, but the one printed by Martin and Spurrell in *The Journal of a Slave Trader* (1962) is still probably the most helpful for the region between the Sierra Leone River and Kittam. We have been able to enrich Newton's narrative in this period from his later recollections in testimony given in 1789 and 1790 to committees of the House of Commons during the abolition campaign. For sources, see the notes below for chapter 11.

Chapter 6

This chapter closely follows Newton's vivid recital in *An Authentic Narrative* of his experience on the *Greyhound*. Newton's personal diary includes an entry for March 21, 1757, that adds further detail by naming Captain Anthony Gother as the master of the *Greyhound*, and this corrects the use of the name Captain Swanwick in many sources. (This error also entered into the historical record through Grace Irwin's biographical novel.) The diary entry in 1757 was the ninth anniversary of the storm at sea where Newton nearly died and where "the Lord was pleased to make the first awakening impressions on my heart." Britain changed to the Gregorian calendar in 1752 and cut out eleven days to catch up, and so thereafter Newton would remember the anniversary of the storm not on the 10th but on the 21st of March. Newton also gave the precise location of the storm in this diary entry as 54 degrees north and 200 leagues west of Ireland, or about 27.5 degrees west. He was exact enough that the site of the storm can now be found on Google maps.

Chapter 7

Newton tells us that it was the first mate of the *Greyhound* who became master of the *Brownlow*. Various records, including the database *Slave Voyages* at https://www.slavevoyages.org/voyage/database, identify this person as Richard Jackson. The cruelties described in this chapter are attributed to Jackson based on recollections from Newton late in life in a letter to the abolitionist Richard Phillips, recorded in Mary Phillips's biography of her father, *Memoir of the Life of Richard Phillips* (1841). The spiritually significant account of Newton's deeper repentance in the midst of his near-death fever is drawn directly from his autobiography.

Chapter 8

For this chapter we are able to draw not only on Newton's autobiography but also on his published *Letters to a Wife*, 2 vols. (1793), which begins with his correspondence with her in 1750. We also have his spiritual diary and his captain's logbook. Newton's manuscript diary for this period is held at the Firestone Library at Princeton, New Jersey, and Marylynn Rouse has done tremendous work transcribing this and Newton's other diaries, some of which have been published. See further www.johnnewton.org. An edition of the logbook was published and has been referred to already in these notes: *The Journal of a Slave Trader (John Newton) 1750–1754*, ed. Martin and Spurrell (1962). Newton's career as a slave trader and his logbook and diaries have together figured significantly in the work of maritime historians and in accounts of the slave trade and abolition, including Adam Hochschild, *Bury the Chains* (2005), James Walvin, *The Trader, the Owner, the Slave* (2007), and Marcus Rediker, *The Slave Ship* (2008). For the history of the slave trade more widely, there is Hugh Thomas's monumental work, *The Slave Trade: The Story of the Atlantic Slave Trade: 1440–1870* (1999). The narrative in this chapter is from Newton's point of view at the time, but the point of view of those African people who were brutally enslaved and transported is given in important accounts such as *The Interesting Narrative of the Life of Olaudah Equiano or Gustavus Vassa, the African* (1789). Such Afro-Atlantic narratives will be significant for developing antislavery sentiment in later decades.

Chapter 9

For this first decade of Newton's ordained ministry, there is a rich collection of printed and archival sources—including his spiritual diary, hymn texts, sermon notebooks, a vast correspondence—and we have drawn upon these for this chapter. These sources are also the basis for the study of Newton's ministry and theology in Bruce Hindmarsh, *John Newton and the English Evangelical Tradition* (1996), where they are itemized in the bibliography. There is likewise a wealth of detail in the added notes and bibliography by Marylynn Rouse in Cecil, *Life of Newton*, ed. Rouse (2000). *The Works of the Rev. John Newton*, 6 vols. (1808–9) is the place to begin for understanding Newton's ministry, and there are modern editions, including one published by the Banner of Truth (2015). Newton's diary mentions how he made a "funeral turn" to a discourse when there was a corpse laid out in the church, and this was on the same day that he was meeting with the children, so we have reimagined a scene where this could have taken place. The sermon quoted at the beginning of his ministry is verbatim from one of his hand-sewn notebooks. For William Cowper's writings, including his conversion narrative that gives his first-hand account of his mental suffering prior to 1764, we have used the Oxford critical editions: *The Letters and Prose Writings of William Cowper*, ed. King and Ryskamp, 5 vols. (1979–86), and *The Poems of William Cowper*, ed. Baird and Ryskamp, 3 vols. (1980–95). Among the many biographies of the poet, we have drawn on James King, *William Cowper* (1986). Recent scholarship has suggested that Cowper's mental condition was more robust during the early period at Olney and emphasizes that his breakdown in 1773 came as a surprise. We have sought to strike a balance between this and the more traditional but perhaps romantic view of him as a constantly "stricken deer." Yet, there were certainly hints in 1772, and perhaps earlier, of his own suffering to come. On the background to mental suffering generally in the eighteenth century, see Roy Porter, *Mind Forg'd Manacles: A History of Madness in England from the Restoration to the Regency* (1987). Newton's diary entry for January 1, 1773, when he wrote "Amazing Grace," and the text of his sermon that day, are transcribed by Marylynn Rouse at www.johnnewton.org. The sermon text is also reprinted in Cecil, *Life of Newton*, ed. Rouse (2000), in an appendix. Newton's funeral sermon for Cowper is reprinted in an appendix as well. "Amazing Grace" and other hymns by Newton and Cowper were published in *Olney Hymns* (1779), and the Cowper-Newton Museum at Olney produced a fine facsimile edition. The museum (www.cowperandnewtonmuseum.org.uk) is also a resource for the local history of Olney as the setting for this chapter. On hymnody in the period, see Donald Davie, *The Eighteenth-Century Hymn* (1993).

Chapter 10

In addition to the sources for the last chapter, we have drawn here upon the narrative of British abolitionism in Adam Hochschild, *Bury the Chains* (2005), and the analysis in Christopher Leslie Brown, *Moral Capital: Foundations of British Abolitionism* (2006). The material curated by Brycchan Carey at www.brycchancarey.com/abolition is a tremendous online resource. John Coffey's work has provided added insight: "Evangelicals, Slavery & the Slave Trade: From Whitefield to Wilberforce," *Anvil* 24, no. 2 (2007): 97–119. The possibility that Newton might have had antislavery concerns well before the 1780s and made his own contribution to the nascent movement is treated judiciously by Coffey in "'I Was an Eye-Witness': John Newton, Anthony Benezet, and the Confession of a Liverpool Slave Trader," *Slavery & Abolition*, published online September 27, 2022. The dialogue between James Albert Ukawsaw Gronniosaw and Newton is based on their encounter as recorded in Newton's diary for November 24, 1772, and the content of *A Narrative of the Most Remarkable Particulars in the Life of James Albert Ukawsaw Gronniosaw, an African Prince, as Related by Himself* (1772). There are archival sources for the relationship between Newton and Wilberforce at the Bodleian Library, Oxford, from the mid-1780s, and we have drawn upon these, as well as from Robert and Samuel Wilberforce's *Life of William Wilberforce*, 5 vols. (1838), and modern biographies of the reformer. The letter of Newton to Wilberforce quoted at the end of this chapter is from November 1, 1787, and it is quoted verbatim from the manuscript in the Bodleian. The larger correspondence is described by Marylynn Rouse in "A Double Portion of My Thoughts and Prayers: John Newton's Letters to William Wilberforce," *Midwestern Journal of Theology* 17, no. 2 (2018): 15–41.

Chapter 11

For this chapter we have followed all the sources quite closely to reconstruct Newton's public contribution to the abolition of the slave trade. Newton's *Thoughts on the African Slave Trade* (1788) is reprinted in *The Journal of a Slave Trader (John Newton) 1750–1754*, ed. Martin and Spurrell (1962). His evidence given to Privy Council in 1789 is recorded in *Reports of the Lords of the Committee of Council Appointed for the Consideration of All Matters Relating to Trade and Foreign Plantations; Submitting . . . the Evidence and Information They Have Collected in Consequence of His Majesty's Order in Council, Dated the 11th of February, 1788, Concerning the Present State of the Trade to Africa, and Particularly the Trade in Slaves* (1789). The questions put to Newton in this session were drawn from Thomas Clarkson, *Questions to be Proposed to Such Gentlemen as Have been Resident on the Coast of Africa . . .* (1788). His testimony before the House Select Committee in 1790 is reported in the *Minutes of the Evidence Taken Before a Committee of the House of Commons, Being a Select Committee, Appointed on the 23d day of April 1790: To Take the Examination of the Several Witnesses Ordered by the House to Attend the Committee of the Whole House, to Whom it is Referred to Consider Further of the Circumstances of the Slave Trade* (1790). We have also quoted from Newton's own handwritten comments written on an abstract of these minutes, published in 1791. The letter to Richard Phillips mentioned in the notes to chapter 7 is quoted here at length. It is from Mary Phillips, *Memoir of the Life of Richard Phillips* (1841). Further material has been consulted from Newton's *Letters to a Wife* (1793). A summary of Newton's contribution to the abolition movement is provided by Marylynn Rouse online at www.brycchancarey.com/abolition/newton.htm. The account of Mary's death is touchingly narrated in Martin, *John Newton* (1950).

Chapter 12

Newton's comment about not being very fond of formal ecclesiastical meetings was made to his friend John Campbell, in *Letters and Conversational Remarks . . . During the Last Eighteen Years of His Life* (1811). An account of Newton's niece Betsy Catlett (later Smith) is provided by Josiah Bull, *John Newton of Olney and St. Mary Woolnoth* (1868) and in Cecil, *Life of Newton*, ed. Rouse (2000). William Bull's remark about Newton being on a voyage as he now approached death is in Josiah Bull, *Memorials of the Rev. William Bull* (1864). Contemporaries began to record their conversations with Newton as he aged, and there are reminiscences, for example, in *The Autobiography of William Jay* (1854). Anecdotes from the end of his life are also reported in Jonathan Aitken, *John Newton* (2007) and in other biographies. In Newton's diary on August 4, 1795, he said memorably that in the face of death he wanted to retire like a thankful guest from a full table. William Jay visited Newton before he died, and later wrote down the words that appear in the final quotation of this chapter.

Epilogue

"The Act for the Abolition of the Slave Trade in 1807" is the final document in Elizabeth Donnan, ed., *Documents Illustrative of the History of the Slave Trade to America, Volume 2: The Eighteenth Century* (1931).

Afterword

Cowper's poem "Charity," quoted here, is from *The Poems of William Cowper, Vol. 1, 1748–1782*, ed. Baird and Ryskamp (1980). Newton's deeply insightful account of a believer's growth in grace over time was originally written in the course of three letters to his friend John Thornton in 1772. It was then published in 1774 in *Twenty-Six Letters on Religious Subjects*. These crowning insights into grace were written and published right around the same time he wrote "Amazing Grace." The letters have been reprinted in *The Life and Spirituality of John Newton*, ed. Hindmarsh (2003).

For Further Reading

Aitken, Jonathan. *John Newton: From Disgrace to Amazing Grace*. Wheaton, IL: Crossway Books, 2007.

A modern biography of Newton by a well-known British author and former politician.

Cecil, Richard. *John Newton*. Edited by Marylynn Rouse. Fearn, Scotland: Christian Focus, 2000.

A reprint of the first biography of Newton, edited with a wealth of detail by the director of the John Newton Project. See also www.johnnewton.org.

Equiano, Olaudah. *The Interesting Narrative and Other Writings*. Edited by Vincent Carretta. Penguin Classics. New York: Penguin Books, 2003.

The most significant African autobiography for the abolition cause, contemporary with Newton.

Hindmarsh, D. Bruce. *John Newton and the English Evangelical Tradition: Between the Conversions of Wesley and Wilberforce*. Grand Rapids, MI: William B. Eerdmans Publishing Company, 2001.

An account of Newton's life and religious thought as an evangelical minister.

Hochschild, Adam. *Bury the Chains: Prophets and Rebels in the Fight to Free an Empire's Slaves*. Boston: Houghton Mifflin, 2005.

An absorbing account of the campaign for abolition in which Newton's story figures significantly.

Newton, John. *Thoughts Upon the African Slave Trade*. London, 1788.

The original text of Newton's key abolitionist tract is available online: https://archive .org/details/thoughtsuponafri00newt.

Newton, John. *The Life and Spirituality of John Newton*. Edited by Bruce Hindmarsh. Vancouver: Regent College Publishing, 2003.

An edition of Newton's original autobiography along with his classic account of growth in grace.

Newton, John. *The Works of John Newton*. 4 vols. Edinburgh: Banner of Truth, 2015.
    A modern reprinting of the collected works of Newton.
Rediker, Marcus. *The Slave Ship: A Human History*. New York: Penguin Books, 2008.
    *A thorough and compassionate history of the Atlantic slave system, drawing in part on
    Newton's involvement, by a leading maritime historian.*
Slave Voyages. "Trans-Atlantic Slave Trade Database," https://www.slavevoyages.org/.
    A comprehensive database built on years of international cooperative scholarship.

About the Authors

Bruce Hindmarsh, DPhil (Oxon), is the James M. Houston Professor of Spiritual Theology and Professor of the History of Christianity at Regent College in Vancouver. He wrote his doctoral thesis at Oxford on John Newton, which was published as *John Newton and the English Evangelical Tradition* (Oxford University Press, 1996). A paperback edition was published by Eerdmans in 2000. He edited and wrote an introduction for an edition of Newton's autobiography and his letters on growth in grace: *The Life and Spirituality of John Newton* (Regent College Publishing, 1998). Bruce speaks and writes regularly for academic and general audiences around the world on history, theology, and the spiritual life. Some of this work and his other books can be viewed at www.brucehindmarsh.com.

Craig Borlase is a *New York Times, Sunday Times,* and international bestselling ghostwriter, collaborating with others to create dramatic, engaging memoirs. Previous work includes *Finding Gobi* (the *New York Times* bestselling account of an ultra-marathon runner's chance encounter with a stray dog in the Mongolian desert) and *My Name Is Tani* (the story of an eight-year-old chess prodigy living in a homeless shelter in NYC, soon to be a Paramount Pictures movie produced by Trevor Noah). His most recent project is a powerful story of redemption about a man sentenced to life for a crime he committed as a child. For more information about Craig and his work, visit www.craigborlase.com.